Shakespeare's Sonnets Exposed

Volume 1: Sonnets I - XXV

Written by **fisher king**

Illustrations by **Gabriel W. Metcalfe**

First edition published in South Africa on the 22nd of January 2020.

Text and illustrations copyright:

© 2020 fisher king / Adam Fisher

sonnetcomix.com

All rights reserved.

| FISHER KING

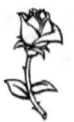

CONTENTS

Preface	1
Introduction	4
A Note Before We Begin	13
The Dedication	16
Sonnet 1	19
Sonnet 2	25
Sonnet 3	30
Sonnet 4	34
Sonnet 5	38
Sonnet 6	43
Sonnet 7	47
Sonnet 8	51
Sonnet 9	56
Sonnet 10	60
Sonnet 11	63
Sonnet 12	68
Sonnet 13	73
Sonnet 14	78
Sonnet 15	83
Sonnet 16	87
Sonnet 17	92

Sonnet 18	98
Sonnet 19	103
Sonnet 20	107
Sonnet 21	115
Sonnet 22	120
Sonnet 23	126
Sonnet 24	134
Sonnet 25	141
Thanks	149
Appendix	151

SHAKESPEARE'S SONNETS EXPOSED: VOLUME 1 |

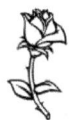

PREFACE

Four centuries ago, a brilliant sorcerer discovered a way to bury his spirit inside a very special book, one that contains a fantastically constructed wilderness of the imagination that has brought immeasurable entertainment and puzzlement to poets and scholars while simultaneously traumatising schoolchildren around the world. In 2012, while studying under the excellent Oxford-trained "Bardologist" Dr. Noam Reisner at Tel Aviv University, I was introduced to and possessed by the Spirit of Shakespeare, and realised that the simple reason that Shakespeare's Sonnets have not inspired as much interest as his plays is that they're too clever for their own good, and are sorely in need of visual representation.

I have subsequently spent an enormous amount of effort attempting to produce a graphic novel adaptation that will render the sonnets accessible and entertaining to all.

As part of my crowdfunding effort, I have been producing a podcast called Shakespeare's Sonnets Exposed, and because I become self-conscious whenever I'm being recorded I've found it necessary to write and follow a script for each episode. It occurred to me, then, that once I've got everything written down anyway I may as well make it available as a reading experience; some might find it easier to follow, others may well find it easier on the ears.

As my compulsion is to right a historical wrong, and shed as much light on Shakespeare's spirit as possible, I'll be happy with whatever gets the message across.

I hope you enjoy reading this as much as I've enjoyed putting it together, and I urge you to consider contributing towards the graphic novel production! Links to do so can be found on the website at **https://www.sonnetcomix.com**.

Thank you for reading!

Adam

(fisher king)

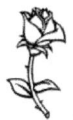

INTRODUCTION

Hamnet and Legacy

William Shakespeare and his father John were heavily invested in the concept of legacy, which a fair number of people in those days were, but John Shakespeare was a particularly ambitious man and in the 1560's or 70's had applied for a coat of arms. This was very important as it would render him a gentleman, with all that being a gentleman entailed which included being able to carry a sword. It might be of interest, then, to learn that back then the only commoners authorised to carry swords were actors and in addition to writing plays William Shakespeare's chosen profession included acting in plays as well.

One important aspect of a coat of arms is that it was passed down from father to son. In those days, women could only bear children, not legacy, and the very idea behind a marriage contract was that the man was effectively buying the rights to a woman's womb so that he could have a son with his name, who could then inherit whatever wealth or titles he was able to amass during his lifetime.

William Shakespeare had three children, two daughters and a son, his son Hamnet being the only child of the three who would be capable of carrying Shakespeare's name and legacy. Unfortunately, Hamnet died in 1596 at the tender age of 11. It is suspected that he died of the black plague, though there has been some speculation about other possibilities, but the important fact here is that his death was devastating to Shakespeare, both as a father who loved his son, and as a man being confronted by the death of his paternal legacy. A few months after Hamnet's death, the Shakespeares were finally awarded their coat of arms - a coat of arms without a son to carry them, which I expect would have been very painful indeed.

The following comment was made on Hamnet Shakespeare's Wikipedia page: "Unlike his contemporary Ben Jonson, who wrote a lengthy piece on the death of his own son, Shakespeare, if he wrote anything in response, did so more subtly". It's interestingly on point, because upon Hamnet's death Shakespeare poured everything that he had into the sonnets, and worked on them for most of the remaining days of his life. He would turn them into a tribute and a memorial to his son, to his legacy, and, effectively, to himself.

Unlike Shakespeare's plays, which we only have in writing because members of his company wanted to put together a memorial for the Bard, Shakespeare himself published Shakespeare's Sonnets, along with the attached poem "A Lover's Complaint". "A Lover's Complaint", incidentally, is a poem describing the experience of reading the sonnets, and it suggests that Shakespeare anticipated and was possibly even relying on their being somewhat misunderstood.

Not only is it the only work of Shakespeare's that he ever published, but it's also the only work of his which has gone largely unnoticed by history. There's almost no mention of criticism for his sonnets from his time, and it's actually difficult to find evidence of people buying it. Roughly thirty years later, in 1640, a man named John Benson republished the sonnets along with other poems in "Shakespeare's Collected Poems", in which he not only reordered the sonnets but also took liberties with the pronouns so that they wouldn't appear to be addressed to a young man.

Until 1780, when Edmond Malone miraculously rescued the original 1609 Quarto edition, Benson's publication stood as the definitive version of Shakespeare's sonnets and so everyone who had read them had been reading a decidedly different set of poems; the influence this has had over current interpretations has never been shaken and the damage to Shakespeare's memory was done; the sonnets are now traditionally analysed as missives, or love letters, to a younger male lover and to an unattractive mistress, and it is due to this that we now think of Shakespeare as having been a pederast - a man sexually attracted to young men - and unfaithful to his wife.

This, in spite of the fact that the original sonnet sequence is all the evidence we could possibly need that neither of these were the case.

This unfaithful reading is also the reason why these sonnets have seemed so confounding and mysterious - when the text is read directly from the pages, consumed "as is", the intention becomes straightforward even though the imagery remains stunningly complex. I believe that what initially allowed me personally to see the sonnets for what they are was sheer naivety, or ignorance, as I arrived at the text with very few preconceptions and from the very first sonnet was inexplicably haunted by a sense of standing over a grave.

When we encounter any sonnet sequence from that period it is of utmost importance to ask what the sonnets are, whose voice they're speaking in, and to whom they are speaking. In this case they were not written to some aristocrat, or noble, or secret lover; they were written to himself, to the memory of his son, to his wife, and to us... to any future reader who would rescue these reflections from the darkness of oblivion.

When one reads these poems as mourning poems, as poems of love and loss and grief, real love for oneself and one's immediate family, the intention of Shakespeare's Sonnets becomes very clear and transforms the mysterious sequence into what is undoubtedly one of the most heartbreakingly tragic and beautiful pieces of writing in the rich history of the English language.

Framing, Originality and Influences

It is important to note that Shakespeare, like other great writers prior to the influence of the Futurists in the early 20th century, did not consider "originality" to be a hallmark of good art and was proud of the process to which he explicitly refers in sonnet 78:

> *Yet be most proud of that which I compile,*
> *Whose influence is thine, and born of thee:*
> *In others' works thou dost but mend the style,*
> *And arts with thy sweet graces graced be;*

Shakespeare's skills did not lie in coming up with "original" stories, but in combining and enhancing existing ones, a technique that he used extensively for both his plays and for his sonnets with the most exquisite skill. Shakespeare's primary influences for producing his sonnets may have been his family and his obsession with legacy, but he drew heavily from a multitude of excellent sources that were available to him: in the following paragraphs I will discuss the Bible and Ovid's Metamorphoses, but that is only because of how essential they are to understanding the framing of the sequence; many of the sonnets have conceits borrowed from or playing against the works of his contemporaries or other stories that would have been circulating in those times.

The Geneva Bible

Throughout the sequence Shakespeare often alludes (and many times quotes) from the Christian Bible, and from what I've read it appears that he was familiar with a number of translations but favoured the Geneva edition.

I am of the opinion that the idea of "love" references the love outlined in Corinthians; I also believe that there might be a connection between sonnet 105's "fair, kind and true" and verse 13's "faith, hope and love": "And now abideth faith, hope and love, even these three: but the chiefest of these is love".

In addition to Shakespeare's biographical inspiration for the sonnets and the Bible, there are two texts in particular that the reader should be familiar with prior to approaching them.

Arthur Golding's Translation of Ovid's Metamorphoses

It has been well-established that in all of his writing, Shakespeare was heavily influenced by Arthur Golding's translation of Ovid's Metamorphoses. While there are many references in the sequence to the Metamorphoses, two of the stories are crucial to understanding the sonnets.

First, Shakespeare's Sonnets are very precisely framed by Golding's version of the tale of Narcissus and Echo, in which Shakespeare is Narcissus, each sonnet is his reflection, and the reader is Echo.

The Narcissus and Echo story is the single thread that connects all of the sonnets in the sequence. In its sonnet sequence form it is the story of Narcissus's love for his reflection, and then his reflection's conversation with Echo, the only witness to this love once Narcissus has died. This may seem a little strange at first, but it becomes much clearer going forward how these elements work together.

Both the original and modern English versions of Golding's translation of Narcissus and Echo are available in the Appendix side by side, along a list of quotes and references made by the sonnets to the Ovidian text.

It has occurred to me that the reason the Narcissus and Echo myth was so well suited to Shakespeare's purpose is that each sonnet is a reflection, not just in the sense of mirroring its author, but also in the sense of its being a thoughtful reflection on death, mourning, love, loss and legacy.

The bottom line is that if you are not familiar with that particular version of the story of Narcissus and Echo, and Golding's language, you're going to miss out on a whole lot of what Shakespeare's sonnets are doing.

Second, throughout the sequence Shakespeare references the sun, the sun god Phoebus, and the seasons; in addition to the constant play on "sun" and "son", these references are directly taken from Golding's translation of the tale of Phaethon, the son of Phoebus.

The tale of Phaethon will be considerably less familiar to modern readers than the tale of Narcissus and Echo. Phoebus is the god who drives the chariot that carries the sun across the sky. On meeting and acknowledging his son for the first time, the sun god unintentionally grants him permission to drive his chariot which he understands will be his son's doom. He is distraught when his son is ultimately killed by Zeus as a punishment for almost bringing about the end of the world.

According to the adjectives used throughout the sequences to describe the seasons, they appear to be referencing the personifications that surround Phoebus when Phaethon meets him in the sun god's palace. Also surrounding Phoebus in his palace are the personifications of the various measurements of time, which are invoked in many ways; as Shakespeare is vicariously travelling through time through the sonnets he has written, time is an important theme to pay attention to as one reads through the sequence.

I warmly recommend this book to all Shakespeare fans and scholars - Arthur Golding's translation of Ovid's Metamorphoses was published in 1904 as "Shakespeare's Ovid" and is available for free from **openlibrary.org** and **http://archive.org/details/shakespearesovid00oviduoft**. You may notice that Ovid translated the book's title as "Metamorphosis", which is unconventional and why I tend to confuse the singular and the plural when referring to it.

The Phoenix and the Turtle

Shakespeare's 1601 poem, unofficially titled "The Phoenix and the Turtle", is described by its Wikipedia entry as "an allegorical poem about the death of ideal love by William Shakespeare" that is "widely considered to be one of his most obscure works and has led to many conflicting interpretations."

Once the theme of Shakespeare's Sonnets is understood, it becomes readily apparent that "The Phoenix and the Turtle" is, in fact, a precursor to the sonnet sequence. The poem describes both the death of Hamnet and the death of William Shakespeare himself: Shakespeare is the turtledove, Hamnet is the phoenix, and once the phoenix has died it is to be born again in the form of everlasting poetry.

Number Puzzles

It is my estimation that Shakespeare's Sonnets are the product of at least a decade of labour, and there are many well-documented points of interest where numbers in the sonnets refer to the numbers of the sonnets. I have discussed the connections I've read about or made myself, but I'm very confident that I have missed plenty more than I've spotted.

Sonnet Editions

It was only after working on Sonnet 16 that I came to realise just how problematic the modernised text of the sonnets is, and since discovering that I have made a point of using the original 1609 Quarto text exclusively, only referencing the modernised text when I get stuck. The glaringly obvious line from sonnet 16 is line 10:

> "Which this (Times pensel or my pupill pen)"

which in the modernised edition has been replaced with

> "Which this, Time's pencil, or my pupil pen,"

and while re-formatting sonnet 2, I realised that line 10 and 11's

> "If thou couldst answer 'This fair child of mine
> Shall sum my count, and make my old excuse,'"

have introduced the apostrophes which do not appear in the original text. This shuts down any alternate reading of those lines. I'm also concerned by the treatment of the second line of sonnet 146, which is considered an "obvious" typo when I'm convinced that the chances of that having occurred are highly unlikely.

While both the original and modernised text are available from **shakespeares-sonnets.com**, I personally prefer the free, high-quality, searchable scans of the original 1609 Quarto available from **https://archive.org/details/shakespearessonn00shakrich**.

For the purposes of this book, I will introduce each Sonnet with its original text, but use modernised text in the analysis to make it easy for the reader to follow along. Where the modernised text differs significantly from the original, I will attempt to correct those differences myself.

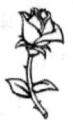

A NOTE BEFORE WE BEGIN

Shakespeare's Sonnets do not work when read out of sequence. Each sonnet builds on its predecessors, and there are aspects of the early sonnets that only become apparent when later sonnets refer back to them. Certain statements that I make about the first sonnet, for example, might seem like a real stretch until we get to the later sonnets, but you can rest assured that I'll always provide evidence and show my work where practical.

The good news is that with just the background provided from the introduction and this note you'll be more than ready to take on the sonnets without a guide and still have a pretty good idea of what's going on.

I find it helpful to begin our journey into the sonnets with a quote from sonnet 24:

> *Now see what good-turns eyes for eyes have done,*
> *Mine eyes have drawn thy shape, and thine for me*
> *Are windows to my breast, where-through the Sun*
> *Delights to peep, to gaze therein on thee*

What Shakespeare is saying here is that the eyes are the windows to the soul, and in Arthur Golding's version of Narcissus and Echo, Narcissus' bright, twinkling eyes, often referred to as stars, are of great importance.

Even though the sonnets were originally numbered with Arabic numerals, I like the fact that it's become traditional to print them using roman numerals so that the "i", "ii", "iii" that label sonnets 1, 2 and 3 now title each sonnet in a way that suggests that it is both an "eye", or window into (and out of) Shakespeare's soul, and also an "I", an identification or a representation of Shakespeare himself. The latter, of course, is purely my own invention, but it is also suggested by the distinct difference of the original text's spelling of the word "eyes" in the original text, where the first line is actually "Now see what good-turns eyes for eies have done".

It's also important to note here that when he writes "where-through the sun / delights to peep" he is also referencing his lost son, Hamnet, whose cherished memory he harbours in his breast. The word "sonnet" means "little song", a meaning which Shakespeare alludes to often, but it also suggests "little son", a replacement for Hamnet that will carry the Bard's legacy to you, the reader.

THE DEDICATION

1609 QUARTO VERSION

SHAKE-SPEARES
SONNETS,
Neuer before Imprinted.

TO.THE.ONLIE.BEGETTER.OF.
THESE.INSVING.SONNETS.
M^r.W.H. ALL.HAPPINESSE.
AND.THAT.ETERNITIE.
PROMISED.
BY.
OVR.EVER-LIVING.POET.
WISHETH.
THE.WELL-WISHING.
ADVENTVRER.IN.
SETTING.
FORTH.

T.T.

ANALYSIS

Determining the correct place to discuss the dedication was far from a trivial task, and although I've settled on positioning it here, preceding the sonnets, it must be noted that there's a good reason that I only discussed it in the seventh episode of the podcast: it really does require some familiarity with the themes established in the sequence. If you're finding my explanations here strange or unbelievable, I recommend skipping ahead to sonnet 1 and returning to it later.

The two pages introducing the original 1609 Quarto edition, the title page and the dedication, have baffled scholars and fans for centuries, giving rise to many fanciful theories.

It is my opinion that Shakespeare and his publisher, Thomas Thorpe, worked very closely together to ensure that there were no errors or misprints in the sonnet sequence, and that Thorpe would have been the one and only person who we could be certain would know what the sequence was about. With that in mind, I am quite convinced that Thorpe used his dedication as an opportunity to provide a hint to the reader.

The title page says "SHAKE-SPEARE'S SONNETS", "Never before Imprinted". "Never before Imprinted" is significant because some of Shakespeare's sonnets had already been circulated against his wishes prior to their 1609 publication; this line informs the reader that this is the definitive edition.

"The only begetter" of these sonnets is Mr W. H., which I believe to be either "William Himself" or a conflation of the names "William" and "Hamnet", the father and son reflections that have created and inspired the sonnet sequence.

"Insuing", an obsolete form of "ensuing", ties in to the legal theme that runs throughout the sequence.

"All happiness" is the happiness described in sonnet 6, and the "eternity promised" by the "ever-living poet" is the journey into posterity that Shakespeare has promised himself, the poet who will live forever buried in the sonnets which are his last Will and testament.

The "well-wishing adventurer" is Shakespeare's spirit, embedded in the sonnet sequence, as well as the reader. Not only is Thorpe calling the "adventurer" well-intentioned, but he appears to be referring to the well in which Narcissus sees his reflection. This suggests that the adventurer is Shakespeare's spirit reflected in the poetry, granting its creator's wish to live on for posterity, and also the reader who is embarking on their own adventure into the imagined world of the sonnets, in turn granting the sonnets' wish to breathe new life into them and recall their creator from the grave.

"Setting", in my opinion, was intended as a pun, referring to the setting of the type in the printing press, the sonnets setting forth on their journey into the darkness of the unknown future, and the reader departing on their journey into the beautiful, dark depths of Shakespeare's soul.

SONNET 1

1609 QUARTO VERSION

FRom faireſt creatures we deſire increaſe,
That thereby beauties Roſe might neuer die,
But as the riper ſhould by time deceaſe,
His tender heire might beare his memory:
But thou contracted to thine owne bright eyes,
Feed'ſt thy lights flame with ſelfe ſubſtantiall fewell,
Making a famine where aboundance lies,
Thy ſelfe thy foe,to thy ſweet ſelfe too cruell:
Thou that art now the worlds freſh ornament,
And only herauld to the gaudy ſpring,
Within thine owne bud burieſt thy content,
And tender chorle makſt waſt in niggarding:
Pitty the world,or elſe this glutton be,

To eate the worlds due,by the graue and thee.

ANALYSIS

From fairest creatures we desire increase,
That thereby beauty's Rose might never die,
But as the riper should by time decease,
His tender heir might bear his memory:

Beauty, throughout the sonnet sequence, refers to Shakespeare and his creative store of wonderful ideas and words. Beauty's rose is both the sonnet that is planted on the page, and the sonnet sequence in its entirety.

The well-understood reference that's being made in the first two lines is to "husbandry", meaning farming, where we breed the best stock of our animals and crops, but the word we need to look at more closely is "creatures". In Old French "creatures" meant "women", which in this context would be the sonnet pages as well as the readers of the sonnets, and the word is also used in the sense of "things that are created", in particular referring to the best ideas, words, and works that Shakespeare has to draw on. The "we" that desires increase is the general "we", but also the sonnets of the sonnet sequence - and so the sonnets desire to be increased by the fairest creations of Shakespeare's mind in order to preserve themselves.

"The riper" means the older, or more mature, which would be both the physical Shakespeare and the earlier sonnets in the sequence. Shakespeare will physically die in time, but his sonnets will experience a different kind of death as the reader moves on to the later sonnets and forgets the earlier ones.

The "tender heir", the sonnet version of Shakespeare, will carry his memory forward even when his physical body is gone. "Tender" here means soft, and gentle, and younger, but from the middle of the 16th century the word also meant to formally offer a plea, evidence, or money to discharge a debt. This last meaning fits well with the language of spending and lending in sonnet 4, and with this in mind the sonnets become Shakespeare's heirs that he is lending to the reader, and using to pay off his debt to Hamnet, his lost son.

But thou contracted to thine own bright eyes,
Feed'st thy light's flame with self-substantial fuel,
Making a famine where abundance lies,
Thy self thy foe, to thy sweet self too cruel:

Contracted here has three different meanings. The first, and most straightforward, is "legally obliged", in particular being bound by the written word. The second meaning in Shakespeare's day was "married", which refers to the relationship of Narcissus to his reflection, and the third meaning is to be made smaller. In the sequence we experience Shakespeare shrinking himself, shrinking his spirit into these 154 sonnets, or "little songs", summarising himself, or 154 aspects of himself, into 154 "eyes", 154 windows into his soul.

"Thy light's flame" is a reference to Cupid's fire from the Narcissus tale, which is the burning love that Narcissus has for his reflection, and that love is what Shakespeare has for himself, for his son, for his work, the sonnets, and even for the reader, without whom his efforts here would be in vain; we see this in the famous sonnet 130, "My mistress 'eyes are nothing like the sun;", his declaration that although the reader isn't physically attractive, his love for her is truer than that which any other man has lied to her about.

What Shakespeare is doing when writing the sonnets is burning his own love in order to fuel more love, investing himself in this literal labour of love in which the more love he shares the more he expects to get in return. Whether he began writing these sonnets in 1593 when Marlowe died, or in 1596 when Hamnet died, the sonnet sequence became his life's work and he poured everything he had into it, especially because after Hamnet died he had no-one else to share his legacy with.

On the other side of the sonnet looking glass, the sonnets are doing the feeding. If we think of Narcissus' reflection being "self substantial", or made of Narcissus, the reflection was feeding Narcissus's burning desire. Simultaneously, the sonnets must beget, or inspire, other sonnets if Shakespeare or the sonnets are to exist for posterity.

All of these words and thoughts are Shakespeare's lifeblood, and in the graphic novel I use the image of him pricking himself and bleeding into the open mouth of his waiting sonnet reflection. Metaphorically speaking, Shakespeare's blood flowed black with the ink of unwritten words, words that needed to be expressed or else be buried with his physical body when he died.

Shakespeare is feeding the sonnets his lifeblood, and they will leave a creative void when they are done. The sonnets are to Shakespeare as the water's reflection is to Narcissus, a cruel enemy that takes but does not give, an untouchable lover. This image holds even as we switch to the other side of the mirror. The sonnets are taking the love from Shakespeare that was due the world, love that rightly belonged to his son, to his family, and to the audiences of his plays.

Another reading of lines 7 and 8 is that by turning his personal tragedy into sonnets, Shakespeare is being cruel to himself by indulging and wallowing in his grief far longer and far more profoundly than might be considered natural.

> *Thou that art now the world's fresh ornament,*
> *And only herald to the gaudy spring,*
> *Within thine own bud buriest thy content,*
> *And tender churl mak'st waste in niggarding:*

The "fresh ornament" is the sonnet, as it is being written it is full of youth. Art is a very interesting word, because in addition to its use as the older form of the word "are", it can also be read as the verb "to create", introducing a meaning of "you, Shakespeare, who are now creating the world's fresh ornament".

Herald was not only one who announces, or a messenger, but it was also the title given to the thirteen members of the college of arms who could authorise a coat of arms for the Shakespeare family. The Shakespeares' coat of arms was authorised merely three months after Hamnet's death; it is not recorded whether his passing influenced the decision, but in any event the tragic end of the Shakespeare name would render the coat of arms effectively useless.

"The gaudy spring" has two important meanings: the first is that in Golding's language it is the word used to refer to the water in the heavenly clearing in which Narcissus sees his reflection, the second is the seasonal reference that's used throughout the sequence wherein spring represents youth, summer maturity and the prime of life and winter old age and death.

Once the reference to the story of Phaethon is established in sonnet 7, it becomes clear that the seasons referenced in the sequence are the personifications that surround Phoebus when Phaethon meets him for the first time in the sun god's palace.

The rose is Shakespeare's symbol of both sonnet and sonnet sequence. There are two meanings of the word "content" that are significant here. The first is the contents of Shakespeare, who is burying his soul, his inner self, into the bud - that is rose bud - that he is planting on this page. The second is that he is burying his happiness, because he is mourning his son and the loss of his legacy.

At the same time, the sonnet's content is buried within the page, possibly beneath its words in the way that a human's spirit is buried beneath their appearance.

"Niggarding" in Shakespeare's day was used to mean "to be miserly", or "stingy", and here is saying that to keep Shakespeare's inspiration, his son's memory, and his creative legacy to himself would be wasteful and foolish. There is also a suggestion that mourning his loss with sonnets rather than attempting to have another son is selfish and wasteful.

Pity the world, or else this glutton be,
To eat the world's due, by the grave and thee.

The closing couplet is especially ambiguous. For Shakespeare, pitying the world can be both sharing his reflections with his living friends, family and audiences, and creating the sonnets; either way he will be a glutton if he keeps his reflections for himself, whether by recording them in the sequence or not at all. For the sonnet, pitying the world means inspiring another sonnet and not keeping Shakespeare's words to itself; the sonnet is a glutton both for keeping Shakespeare's words from the living world, but also for not sharing them with the rest of the sonnets.

Another coherent reading of the last two lines is this: "pity the world, Shakespeare, or be this sonnet: this sonnet will consume all that you have to offer".

A final possibility is that the reader is being asked to pity the world by giving voice to the sonnets.

"Grave" is a very interesting word choice. It has two additional meanings that we don't often consider, from the Old French "serious", and the Old English "to dig", which foreshadows the "deep trenches" of sonnet 2. Graves and tombs are referenced quite a lot in the sonnet sequence: the sonnet sequence is the grave of Shakespeare's legacy in which the Bard buries his reflections, and the sequence is eternally mourning by the graves of both Shakespeare and Hamnet.

The story of the sonnet sequence takes place beside the grave, just as Narcissus died next to the water; here we read of a Shakespeare beside his son's grave, the sonnets beside their creator's grave, and the reader looking into the grave in which the creator's spirit has been buried.

SONNET 2

1609 QUARTO VERSION

VVHen fortie Winters ſhall beſeige thy brow,
And digge deep trenches in thy beauties field,
Thy youthes proud liuery ſo gaz'd on now,
Wil be a totter'd weed of ſmal worth held:
Then being askt,where all thy beautie lies,
Where all the treaſure of thy luſty daies;
To ſay within thine owne deepe ſunken eyes,
Were an all-eating ſhame,and thriftleſſe praiſe.
How much more praiſe deſeru'd thy beauties uſe,
If thou couldſt anſwere this faire child of mine
Shall ſum my count,and make my old excuſe
Proouing his beautie by ſucceſſion thine.
This were to be new made when thou art ould,
And ſee thy blood warme when thou feel'ſt it could.

ANALYSIS

When forty Winters shall besiege thy brow,
And dig deep trenches in thy beauty's field,
Thy youth's proud livery so gazed on now,
Will be a totter'd weed of small worth held:

Each sonnet begins with the first letter enlarged, and it is interesting to note that when the first letter is a "W" it is sometimes, as here, printed "VV". I believe that the distinction may be intentional, as in French "W" is "double V" and I suspect that this might be an indication of William being separated out into his physical and his textual entities.

Two important terms in this opening quatrain are "besiege" and "trenches", ideas that will come up again in sonnet 5. As an older man, Shakespeare will be able to read these sonnets and see his own youth reflected in their writing, just as a father sees his youth reflected in his son.

At age forty, Shakespeare's brow will be wrinkled, which will show as "trenches" in his skin. For the sonnets, their words are entrenched in the lines across the page and they have a mission to infiltrate the reader's mind which is located behind the brow. Alternatively, and in line with the farming metaphor from sonnet 1, Shakespeare has used his pen to plough furrows along the page in which his words will be cultivated. Each sonnet produces the seeds that will grow into its successor.

The word "livery" came from the Old French for "delivered", and came to mean "servant's clothing" which is still in use today. So the "youth's proud livery" is what younger Shakespeare is delivering to older Shakespeare and the reader - the sonnets - as well as his physical body that clothes his spirit and the words that clothe his intentions.

"Totter'd weed", or "tattered weed", is an interesting image. It's an expression that works as well for worn clothing as it does for crumpled paper, but as the sonnet sequence is represented by the rose, we are here presented with an image of a young, proud rose contrasted with a tattered weed. What Shakespeare and the reader are holding is the sonnet that reflects Shakespeare as he was when he wrote it, but time will pass and the sonnet will become like its creator, used and discarded. This is only the second sonnet, by the time Shakespeare produces a fortieth he expects that he will look back on this one as old and obsolete. Additionally, by the time the reader gets to the fortieth sonnet he probably won't be sparing this one much thought, either.

> *Then being asked, where all thy beauty lies,*
> *Where all the treasure of thy lusty days;*
> *To say within thine own deep sunken eyes,*
> *Were an all-eating shame, and thriftless praise.*

"Lies" has two meanings here, the first being in the sense of one's final resting place. Hamnet is in the grave, eventually Shakespeare will be too, and his spirit will be buried in the sonnets. The treasure of Shakespeare's lusty days was Hamnet, and the lusty days themselves, the latter being what he is now investing in the sonnets. The lusty days of the sonnets, however, are the days when Shakespeare was alive; just like Narcissus' reflection, once Narcissus dies the reflection's lusty days will be over.

The word "treasure" is fascinating - it means the same thing that we use it for today, a quantity of valuable objects, but is derived from the greek word "thesaurus" which also means "storehouse". Shakespeare's treasure, the sonnet sequence, is a storehouse containing his reflections, his spirit, and his most valuable words.

The expressions "deep sunken" and "all-eating" evoke an image of worms eating a body in the grave. The "deep sunken eyes" refer to Shakespeare's reflection in the sonnets: where Narcissus' reflection is submerged in water, Shakespeare's is submerged in ink and parchment. If Shakespeare were to tell people that his spirit, his son and his legacy were buried in the pages of the sonnet sequence it would be shameful, just as if the second sonnet were to consume his words without preceding more sonnets.

That would be terrible; but at the same time, for Shakespeare to say that his all had been invested in the sonnet sequence might be wonderful praise for the sonnets, perhaps even excessive. "Thriftless" implies "wasteful", "waste" being a term repeated quite a few times throughout the sequence, and "praise" in Shakespeare's day meant "to attach a value to". To read these lines with Shakespeare as the one being interrogated, if he were to answer that his treasure was in his own eyes - as opposed to in his son's or his sonnets' - that would indeed be shameful and narcissistic.

> *How much more praise deserv'd thy beauty's use,*
> *If thou couldst answer this fair child of mine*
> *Shall sum my count, and make my old excuse*
> *Proving his beauty by succession thine.*

Shakespeare's "beauty" is not physical, but intellectual and emotional. "Beauty's use" is the sonnet sequence, not only is it Shakespeare's beauty given form by the sonnet, but it is also the sonnet being given function by the reader.

The sonnet sequence is the sum of the individual sonnets, and far more important and valuable than the sonnets is their combination; as I've stated earlier, the sonnets simply cannot operate in isolation, they must be read together and in sequential order as a single body of work; they are the representatives and the embodiments of Shakespeare himself and they tell a story that has a beginning, a middle and an end. The expression "sum my count" also anticipates the language of "auditing" in sonnet 4, and it appears that in other places, like the play "Othello", Shakespeare has used the word "count" to refer to Judgement Day.

The word "excuse" meant, and still means, "to free from blame". This sonnet will literally make Shakespeare's excuse for him, excusing his lack of a son by serving in his son's place.

"Deserved" meant "served well", so in this sense Shakespeare is serving his sonnet self, his son, and his legacy by answering "this fair child of mine". Shakespeare will be "proving", or demonstrating, his beauty in the sonnets, both by writing it into sonnet 2 and by continuing to produce more sonnets.

Another way to read this quatrain is with "thou" referring to "beauty's use", the sonnet. With that in mind, "How much more praise deserv'd thy beauty's use, / If thou couldst answer 'This fair child of mine'" is saying to the sonnet that it would deserve even more praise if it were to have a succeeding sonnet to answer with.

It is important to note that the apostrophes were not present in the 1609 Quarto edition, and while they are based on the natural sounding of the verse they detract as much as they add. Without the apostrophes, we can read "If thou couldst answer this, fair child of mine", which makes sense as Shakespeare's fair child, the sonnet, would be answering on his behalf and demonstrating his worth.

This were to be new made when thou art old,
And see thy blood warm when thou feel'st it cold.

Each sonnet is, like a child to a parent, a copy, an iteration, so when an older sonnet sees a younger it will be reminded of when it was fresh and relevant - or when the reader moves on to a newer sonnet they will be presented with a younger, fresher sonnet than the one they were reading before.

For Shakespeare, and for the reader, the old sonnets will be a window through which we can view Shakespeare's youth. As ink is the blood of the sonnets, it is cold when it is dry but what we see in the words is a frozen image of the moment when the ink was warm and being drawn across the page by the quill.

SONNET 3

1609 QUARTO VERSION

Looke in thy glaſſe and tell the face thou veweſt,
Now is the time that face ſhould forme an other,
Whoſe freſh repaire if now thou not reneweſt,
Thou doo'ſt beguile the world, vnbleſſe ſome mother.
For where is ſhe ſo faire whoſe vn-eard wombe
Diſdaines the tillage of thy huſbandry?
Or who is he ſo fond will be the tombe,
Of his ſelfe loue to ſtop poſterity?
Thou art thy mothers glaſſe and ſhe in thee
Calls backe the louely Aprill of her prime,
So thou through windowes of thine age ſhalt ſee,
Diſpight of wrinkles this thy goulden time.
But if thou liue remembred not to be,
Die ſingle and thine Image dies with thee.

ANALYSIS

Look in thy glass and tell the face thou viewest
Now is the time that face should form an other;
Whose fresh repair if now thou not renewest,
Thou dost beguile the world, unbless some mother.

"Glass" means mirror, but within the framing of the Narcissus story refers to the surface of the water, or spring, wherein Narcissus sees his reflection. In this case, it also means the ink in which Shakespeare sees his reflection. The sonnet sequence is kind of like Alice's looking glass - the world on the viewer's side of the glass may be real, but what the reflection experiences is its own reality from which it sees the real as its reflection.

What's happening here is that Shakespeare is instructing the sonnet to tell him to write another sonnet, but at the same time the sonnet, which is Shakespeare's reflection, is instructing its maker to tell the sonnet to create another one. As usual, there's the third actor, the reader, being instructed simultaneously to do the same, which means both reading the sonnet (and the subsequent sonnets) and bearing physical children.

Not only will Shakespeare and his sonnet be cheating the world out of a new sonnet if they fail to produce one, but the word "unbless" is very particular. To be unblessed doesn't simply mean to be deprived, or to be made unhappy; it means to remove an existing source of happiness. Shakespeare and his wife were "unblessed" when Hamnet died, and not writing the sonnets - which are a tribute to Hamnet that take over from him in continuing Shakespeare's legacy and spirit - would be an insult to both parents and their lost child's memory.

Sonnet 8's trinity of "sire and child and happy mother" are Shakespeare, the sonnet and the reader, with the reader presumed to be female, playing the role of Echo from the Narcissus story. Here in sonnet 3 we have two references to mother, and the reader - or unblessed mother - could refer to either Shakespeare's wife, Hathaway unblessed with her actual child, or the reader unblessed with more sonnets.

> *For where is she so fair whose un-eared womb*
> *Disdains the tillage of thy husbandry?*
> *Or who is he so fond will be the tomb*
> *Of his self love, to stop posterity?*

In the 16th and 17th century the biology of procreation wasn't well understood, and they believed that a man's semen was planted in an empty womb. Each blank page, each unwritten sonnet, is a womb, and there's a theme beginning with sonnet 8 in which the sonnets - the word literally meaning little songs - are "un-eared" and literally do not have ears to hear even though the reader will sound them out while reading. These lines evoke a very neat image of lines of ink across the page being the rows in which the poet plants his words.

These next two lines are asking if Shakespeare is so greedy for his self-love that he would be prepared to end his legacy by not using it to produce children or sonnets. At the same time, they're asking if the sonnet is so greedy for Shakespeare's self-love that it would be willing to end his legacy by not passing it on to another sonnet.

> *Thou art thy mother's glass and she in thee*
> *Calls back the lovely April of her prime;*
> *So thou through windows of thine age shalt see,*
> *Despite of wrinkles this thy golden time.*

In this second reference to mother, we can imagine that whoever the mother may be, when she looks into these sonnet reflections she will find her youth, and possibly memories of her lost child, buried there.

In sonnet three the word "glass" appears for the first time and is repeated twice, and I believe that in addition to referencing the water reflection of Narcissus, it is also referencing the first Corinthians, chapter 13 verse 12: "For now we see through a glass darkly: but then shall we see face to face. Now I know in part: but then shall I know even as I am known".

When Shakespeare is old, he will look back through these sonnet windows and see his youth in spite of his physical wrinkles. The reader, in whatever age she finds herself reading the sonnets, will look back through the torn and crumpled pages to see Shakespeare's youth.

> *But if thou live remembered not to be,*
> *Die single and thine Image dies with thee.*

The capitalisation of the word "Image" is interesting, not only does it connect us directly to sonnet 24's Image but also to the description of Narcissus' reflection in Golding's translation of Ovid's Metamorphoses.

If Shakespeare lives and does not invest in his legacy, he will die lonely and his imagined reflections will disappear along with his body. If the sonnets live on, but are not remembered, it would amount to the same thing.

SONNET 4

1609 QUARTO VERSION

VNthrifty louelineſſe why doſt thou ſpend,
  Vpon thy ſelfe thy beauties legacy?
Natures bequeſt giues nothing but doth lend,
  And being franck ſhe lends to thoſe are free:
Then beautious nigard why dooſt thou abuſe,
  The bountious largeſſe giuen thee to giue?
Profitles vſerer why dooſt thou vſe
  So great a ſumme of ſummes yet can'ſt not liue?
For hauing traffike with thy ſelfe alone,
  Thou of thy ſelfe thy ſweet ſelfe doſt deceaue,
Then how when nature calls thee to be gone,
  What acceptable Audit can'ſt thou leaue?
    Thy vnuſ'd beauty muſt be tomb'd with thee,
    Which vſed liues th'executor to be.

ANALYSIS

Unthrifty loveliness, why dost thou spend
Upon thy self thy beauty's legacy?
Nature's bequest gives nothing but doth lend,
And being frank she lends to those are free:

"Spend upon thy self" has been understood to mean masturbation, but throughout the sonnet sequence Shakespeare uses the word "spend" very consistently, a great example coming from sonnet 100: "Spend'st thou thy fury on some worthless song". What Shakespeare is spending is time from his remaining days on earth, the passion and love that he has left over that should have been his son's inheritance, and his spirit and philosophy. Shakespeare is treating his soul, his life-force, as currency, he is a wallet filled with words and ideas and he must consider carefully how he spends them.

Due to the nature of the sonnets being Shakespeare's reflection, the meaning of the opening two lines becomes ambiguous: is Shakespeare being selfish by writing the sonnets, which is how he spends his beauty's legacy, or is he being selfish by not writing the sonnets and keeping his legacy for himself?

In addition to the obvious meaning, in the sonnet sequence the feminine word "nature" often appears to refer to Shakespeare, the author of the sonnets. The word derives from the Latin word "natura", meaning "birth", "nature" or "quality". Each sonnet is born, according to the theme of childbearing established in the previous sonnets, and the sonnets espouse Shakespeare's nature, his personality; nature is ever changing and evolving whereas the sonnets are static.

The word "bequest" is derived from the English "bequeath", to leave legacy by a will, and the Old English "about speech", which is an interesting source for a word meaning inheritance but if it's relevant, plays into the sonnets' function as inducing speech in the reader.

In Middle English "frank" meant both "free" and "generous".

So with the meanings of these words contextualised, it becomes apparent that Shakespeare is not giving his spirit to the sonnet, but lending it, and is lending it on the condition that the sonnet will share it, both with the subsequent sonnets and with the reader.

> *Then, beauteous niggard why dost thou abuse*
> *The bounteous largess given thee to give?*
> *Profitless usurer why dost thou use*
> *So great a sum of sums yet canst not live?*

"Sum of sums" prepares us for the word "audit" in the following quatrain, and recalls "This fair child of mine / Shall sum my count" from sonnet 2, ultimately referring to the sonnet sequence. The sonnet sequence is the sum of sonnets, each sonnet being a sum of words and lines and ideas.

Shakespeare is the "beauteous niggard", the miser, if he doesn't share his beauty with the sonnet and the world; the sonnet is miserly if it doesn't share the spirit of its creator by inspiring another sonnet. Neither Shakespeare nor the sonnet profits directly from the usury, or loaning, both because Shakespeare will be dead when the sonnets are read, and because the sonnets cannot live autonomously.

> *For having traffic with thy self alone,*
> *Thou of thy self thy sweet self dost deceive:*
> *Then how when nature calls thee to be gone,*
> *What acceptable* **Audit** *canst thou leave?*

The capitalised and italicised "Audit" comes from the word "hearing", which is an interesting word because each sonnet, or "little song", must be read aloud in order for it to take effect. The sonnets cannot communicate without Echo, the reader, sounding out the words. If Shakespeare doesn't lend the sonnet his beauty, there will be no "audit" when he dies; when Shakespeare sees his sonnets off by publishing them, what effect will they have if they're not read?

> *Thy unused beauty must be tombed with thee,*
> *Which used lives th' executor to be.*

Any unwritten work will be buried with Shakespeare, and any unread sonnets will be buried in the sequence, but if these sonnets are both written and read, they will come alive to serve as the executors of Shakespeare's "Will".

SONNET 5

1609 QUARTO VERSION

THoſe howers that with gentle worke did frame,
The louely gaze where euery eye doth dwell
Will play the tirants to the very ſame,
And that vnfaire which fairely doth excell:
For neuer reſting time leads Summer on,
To hidious winter and confounds him there,
Sap checkt with froſt and luſtie leau's quite gon.
Beauty ore-ſnow'd and barenes euery where,
Then were not ſummers diſtillation left
A liquid priſoner pent in walls of glaſſe,
Beauties effect with beauty were bereft,
Nor it nor noe remembrance what it was.
But flowers diſtil'd though they with winter meete,
Leeſe but their ſhow,their ſubſtance ſtill liues ſweet.

ANALYSIS

Those hours that with gentle work did frame,
The lovely gaze where every eye doth dwell
Will play the tyrants to the very same,
And that unfair which fairly doth excel:

Sonnet 5 opens with the words "Those hours", and while today the word "hours" holds the particular meaning of a fixed quantity of time, it was originally very flexible and was used to describe periods, traditionally seasons and even years. It is likely that here the intended meaning is seasons and years, with additional reference being made to the figures surrounding Phoebus in his palace, the Greek Horae, which numerically and metaphorically leave us with a lot to consider. There are traditionally three "triads" of the Horae: life and growth, law and order, abundance and prosperity, all established themes in the sonnet sequence.

"The lovely gaze" belongs to Shakespeare, and is framed by the sonnets which have been crafted with many hours of careful work for that purpose. When the sonnets says "every eye", it means a number of things. Firstly, it refers to each sonnet, each one being an eye of the sequence: both "eye" as in the organ we use to see as well as "I" for "individual". Secondly, it refers to Shakespeare, who wrote this sequence full of love and sadness, and gazed upon each sonnet both while writing it and while reviewing it. Thirdly, and perhaps more importantly, it refers to the readers.

"Those hours" "will play tyrants" to the eyes.

In Shakespeare's case, he will be "unfaired" by the time that he invests in the sequence; he will become older, less youthful and will also have less to write because the sonnets will have depleted his creative store. From my reading of "outward fare" in sonnet 16, I suspect that there are many occasions when "fair" implies "faire", from the French for "to do" or "to make", and so here I believe that we can read both "unfair" and "unmake".

Those hours of writing will play tyrants to the sonnets, because once Shakespeare is dead they will miss him and mourn him all the more for having spent so much quality time with him.

As for the reader, the hours of reading (and re-reading, whenever the prophecy of the attached poem "A Lover's Complaint" is fulfilled) will play tyrant to the reader's eyes and mind, not only by controlling the reader in a unidirectional relationship but by wasting their time in an activity which will give them less back than the sonnets expect to gain.

> *For never resting time leads Summer on,*
> *To hideous winter and confounds him there,*
> *Sap checked with frost, and lusty leaves quite gone.*
> *Beauty o'er-snowed and bareness every where,*

Time, throughout the sequence, is a conflation of Father Time (Chronos, or Saturn) and Death (the Grim Reaper). Shakespeare uses the seasons to divide life into four stages, with spring being a metaphor for youth in addition to the water in which Narcissus sees himself reflected, and here the meaning seems clear: Time will take Shakespeare from the prime of his life and leave him to die when he's old, and Shakespeare's death will take the sonnet sequence from their prime into the hideous winter of an eternity with no guarantee of being read.

"Sap" and "lusty leaves" are interesting terms because they follow the rose metaphor of the sonnets with the suggestion that the ink is sap and the pages are leaves. This evokes an image of the pages of the sequence disintegrating in the eternal winter.

"Sap" had a couple of meanings in Shakespeare's day, the obvious one being the sap of a plant but the second being a tunnel, or trench, built to conceal an assailant's approach to a fortified place. This recalls sonnet 2's "dig deep trenches in thy beauty's field" which suggests the words in the lines of the sonnets attempting to sneak into the reader's consciousness. "Check" in

Middle English was a word derived from chess and meant "stop or control", and so "sap checked with frost" can be read not only as a rose that doesn't grow - the sonnets - but also as the death of Shakespeare thwarting his attempts to influence or possess the reader.

Every time one encounters "o'er" in the modernised text, it must be understood that it was written "ore" in the original text. Although the modernised reading is usually sensible, the more I encounter it the less correct it seems. Throughout the sonnet sequence, "ore", as in "metalliferous mineral or rock", generally suggests a valuable stone or ink, the ingredients of which included iron sulphate and of which I'm confident that Shakespeare would have been familiar with. It may also imply "beginning", "origin", or "front" from the Old English "or", and possibly even "oral", "of or pertaining to the mouth". Here it suggests that beauty has been snowed over with the ink from Shakespeare's pen.

In the original text, "Those hours" was written "THose howers", a spelling which visually resembles "Those towers", and I cannot help but wonder if there's a possible relationship between the words "towers", "frame", "dwell", "tyrant", "sap", "prisoner", and "walls".

> *Then were not summer's distillation left*
> *A liquid prisoner pent in walls of glass,*
> *Beauty's effect with beauty were bereft,*
> *Nor it nor no remembrance what it was.*

"Summer's distillation" is Shakespeare's spirit distilled into the sonnets, and when we read "a liquid prisoner" we are reminded of Narcissus' reflection looking out from the water, trapped behind "walls of glass"; in other words, Shakespeare's reflection is trapped on the other side of the looking glass. For those of you familiar with the Harry Potter universe, what Shakespeare is describing is very much like the horcruxes that Voldemort creates to achieve immortality.

"Beauty's effect" in this case is the sonnet sequence, and if the sonnets were not recorded then the moment Shakespeare died all of his unwritten ideas and memories would die along with him.

> *But flowers distilled though they with winter meet,*
> *Leese but their show, their substance still lives sweet.*

"Leese" in Middle English meant to "cut", "sever", "separate", "loosen", or "lose"; "substance" meant "being", or "essence".

If Shakespeare were to write himself into the sonnets, his death would be merely the end of his physical body but his essence, having been separated and securely stored, would be released from his fate and continue to live on.

SONNET 6

1609 QUARTO VERSION

THen let not winters wragged hand deface,
In thee thy ſummer ere thou be diſtil'd:
Make ſweet ſome viall;treaſure thou ſome place,
With beauties treaſure ere it be ſelfe kil'd:
That vſe is not forbidden vſery,
Which happies thoſe that pay the willing lone;
That's for thy ſelfe to breed an other thee,
Or ten times happier be it ten for one,
Ten times thy ſelfe were happier then thou art,
If ten of thine ten times refigur'd thee,
Then what could death doe if thou ſhould'ſt depart,
Leauing thee liuing in poſterity?
Be not ſelfe-wild for thou art much too faire,
To be deaths conqueſt and make wormes thine heire.

ANALYSIS

> *Then let not winter's ragged hand deface,*
> *In thee thy summer ere thou be distilled:*
> *Make sweet some vial; treasure thou some place,*
> *With beauty's treasure ere it be self killed:*

This first quatrain continues the distillation image from the previous sonnet. In those days "ragged" meant "rough, shaggy and bristly", which suggests old and wrinkly, and "treasure" is the treasure mentioned in sonnet 2, a storehouse of valuable objects which in this case means Shakespeare's beautiful ideas and the displaced love for his lost son.

While it may not be significant, in the original text "winters" does not have an apostrophe and therefore allows for the possible reading of "Then do not allow ragged hand to deface winters".

The vial is the sonnet, its treasured place the sonnet sequence.

"Self killed" has been modernised to "self-killed", which is one possible reading but it seems plausible that it was also intended to be read "before it becomes the self that is killed".

> *That use is not forbidden usury,*
> *Which happies those that pay the willing loan;*

The "usury" and "willing loan", established in sonnet 4, refer to the act of investing Shakespeare's legacy in the sonnets. "Willing", here, as in most (if not all) of its uses throughout the sequence, is a pun on Shakespeare's name, so the "willing loan" is a loan of Will himself.

> *That's for thy self to breed another thee,*
> *Or ten times happier be it ten for one,*
> *Ten times thy self were happier then thou art,*
> *If ten of thine ten times refigured thee,*

Each sonnet is a little son, a little replacement for Hamnet, who was in turn a little version of Shakespeare. From the farming reference in sonnet 1, Shakespeare is breeding sonnets, and each sonnet's maturation will make Shakespeare happy for having invested in it. If one sonnet can make Shakespeare happy - and if an additional sonnet can make the first sonnet happy - then ten will make them ten times happier; if ten sonnets will make them ten times happier, then a hundred sonnets will do something magical: the word "refigure" is critical here, because with a hundred sonnets Shakespeare will have enough parts of himself to be recognisably "refigured", "reconstructed", and "resurrected".

The numerical significance of this quatrain must not be underestimated, as the simple reading above (one, ten, one hundred) seems to be quite shallow in the shadow of the previous references to hours and seasons.

Then what could death do if thou shouldst depart,
Leaving thee living in posterity?

To "depart" here clearly means to die, with Shakespeare's death being his departure from the physical plane and his leaving the sonnets behind. There's another sense attached, however: by being published, the sonnet sequence is being sent on a journey into the future, into eternity, into the reader's hands wherever and whenever they might be.

This couplet's use of the second person is particularly interesting. "You" are departing, leaving "you" living in posterity. On the one side of the looking glass, Shakespeare is leaving the sonnets and leaving his reflection living on in them; on the other, the sonnets are leaving Shakespeare by being published, and will live on for future generations.

Be not self-willed for thou art much too fair,
To be death's conquest and make worms thine heir.

Recalling "self-killed" from line 4, the accepted modernisation "self-willed" has a similar meaning: if Shakespeare keeps his words to himself, it is a form of suicide; if he dies without publishing the sonnets, it will be a final death and the readers will not be able to resurrect him. The second meaning of "self-willed", in which the Bard plays on his own name, makes this couplet an instruction to Shakespeare to not keep himself to himself, and reinforces the sense that to do so would be suicide.

Having said all that, the original text reads "Be not self-wild", and "wild" in Shakespeare's day meant "uncultivated or desolate region", "in the natural state", "uncultivated", "untamed", "undomesticated" and "uncontrolled". The general sense of the couplet is retained, but there's an additional suggestion of "Shakespeare's spirit must not remain untamed and should be cultivated into more sonnets".

The word "art" here works just like it did in sonnet 1's "Thou that art now": not only is Shakespeare too beautiful for death, but so is the result of his art, the sonnets.

What these final lines are saying is that by being selfless and lending his spirit to the sonnets, Shakespeare will be protected from death; the sonnets are an act of defiance against time and nature that will ensure that the worms will not be the only heirs to his legacy.

SONNET 7

1609 QUARTO VERSION

LOe in the Orient when the gracious light,
Lifts vp his burning head, each vnder eye
Doth homage to his new appearing sight,
Seruing with lookes his sacred maiesty,
And hauing climb'd the steepe vp heauenly hill,
Resembling strong youth in his middle age,
Yet mortall lookes adore his beauty still,
Attending on his goulden pilgrimage:
But when from high-most pich with wery car,
Like feeble age he reeleth from the day,
The eyes(fore dutious)now conuerted are
From his low tract and looke an other way:
So thou, thy selfe out-going in thy noon:

Vnlok'd on diest vnlesse thou get a sonne.

ANALYSIS

Lo! in the Orient when the gracious light,
Lifts up his burning head, each under eye
Doth homage to his new appearing sight,
Serving with looks his sacred majesty,

"The gracious light" in the East refers to the sun-god Phoebus, and "LOe" in the original text can be read both as "Lo!", the shortened form of "look!" or "see!", and as "low", qualifying the position of the sun at sunrise. As always in the sequence, references to the sun also refer to Shakespeare's son, Hamnet, but in this instance also refers to the reader who both literally and figuratively throws light on the sonnets in order to read them.

The "under eyes", those under the sun, can refer to the eyes of the Bard, the sonnet reflections, or the reader.

"New-appearing sight" is interesting, because Shakespeare's sonnet reflections always appear new, even when they're old or have been read before, just as the sun appears new at the beginning of each day; the reader's sight is also new-appearing, probably because the sonnets are static and have no memory of being read before.

In Middle English, the word "homage" referred to the ceremony of a vassal declaring himself his lord's servant, and a "vassal", a servant or young squire, denotes an apprentice. With this in mind, the sun rising in the east is the reader's eye, or the light falling on the opening page; each "under eye", or sonnet, declares himself for Shakespeare and the reader whenever it is read, regardless of who is doing the reading.

Simultaneously, each sonnet does homage to the memory of Shakespeare's son, Hamnet, who appears anew in each one.

From the other side of the sonnet looking glass, when the "gracious light" of the reader lifts up the burning head of the sonnet, each reader's eye reading the sonnet declares itself the sonnet's servant, or at the very least subjects itself to the ideas of each sonnet during the act of reading.

Either way, "serving with looks" is very important; neither Shakespeare, the sonnets, nor the reader are served if the sonnets are not read.

> *And having climbed the steep up heavenly hill,*
> *Resembling strong youth in his middle age,*
> *Yet mortal looks adore his beauty still,*
> *Attending on his golden pilgrimage:*

"Heavenly hill" refers to the location of the spring in which Narcissus sees his reflection. "Resembling" suggests "re-assembling".

"His middle age" could be a number of things. Shakespeare is embedding his youth in the sonnets, as well as the memories of his son, while he is writing in his middle age. If sonnet 7 describes the reading of the sequence, or even the reading of just a single sonnet, then the middle age might refer to the reader experiencing the middle of the sequence, or the middle of the current sonnet. If my latter supposition is correct, then it's more likely that sonnet 7 is specifically describing the act of reading sonnet 7.

"Adore" comes from Old French and Latin meaning to "worship" or "pray", in particular prayer by speech. So here we see living beings worshipping beauty - which in sonnet parlance means Shakespeare and Shakespeare's ideas and creative powers - both by reading the sonnets and by speaking their words out loud.

"Attending" comes from the Old French "atendre", and in Middle English meant to apply one's mind or efforts.

"Golden" takes us back to sonnet 3's "this thy golden time", Shakespeare's youth captured in the sonnets.

"Pilgrimage" takes us back to the dedication of the sonnet sequence and sonnet 6's "departure"; it refers to the sacred journey that the sonnet sequence must undertake after the death of Shakespeare's physical death.

Bearing all of that in mind, what we're seeing in the second quatrain is that reading the sonnets out loud is a form of prayer, and by praying in this way we are applying, or lending, our energies to the "golden pilgrimage", which is the sonnets' sacred journey through eternity.

> *But when from high-most pitch, with weary car,*
> *Like feeble age he reeleth from the day,*
> *The eyes ('fore duteous) now converted are*
> *From his low tract and look an other way:*

"Pitch" meant "slope, degree or inclination", "car" refers to Phoebus' chariot, to "reel" connoted swaying, rocking and being unsteady; "tract" meant both "track" or "course" and "a little book"; all this comes together to describe the weakening of the sun towards the end of the day and the eyes no longer looking in his direction, which describes the effect of reading on the sonnets: if the reader becomes weary and looks away, or turns the page, or closes the book, then the sonnets will cease to serve their master as the reader ceases to serve the sonnets.

> *So thou, thy self out-going in thy noon:*
> *Unlooked on diest unless thou get a son.*

Shakespeare, at the mid-point of his life, is dying without his son to continue his legacy or without the sonnets to replace him. Sonnet 7 is dying without a new sonnet to replace it to keep the reader's attention. The sonnet sequence is dying without a reader to play the part of the sun god.

SONNET 8

1609 QUARTO VERSION

MVſick to heare,why hear'ſt thou muſick ſadly,
Sweets with ſweets warre not ,ioy delights in ioy:
Why lou'ſt thou that which thou receauſt not gladly,
Or elſe receau'ſt with pleaſure thine annoy ?
If the true concord of well tuned ſounds,
By vnions married do offend thine eare,
They do but ſweetly chide thee , who confounds
In ſingleneſſe the parts that thou ſhould'ſt beare:
Marke how one ſtring ſweet husband to an other,
Strikes each in each by mutuall ordering;
Reſembling ſier,and child, and happy mother,
Who all in one,one pleaſing note do ſing:
Whoſe ſpeechleſſe ſong being many,ſeeming one,

Sings this to thee thou ſingle wilt proue none.

ANALYSIS

This is one of my favourite sonnets, because it's one of the clearer keys that Shakespeare provides for the reader. As I've stated before, the word sonnet literally means "little song", and each sonnet is both a "little song" and a "little son", a reflection of Shakespeare and a replacement for Shakespeare's lost son, Hamnet.

> *Music to hear, why hear'st thou music sadly,*
> *Sweets with sweets war not, joy delights in joy:*
> *Why lov'st thou that which thou receiv'st not gladly,*
> *Or else receiv'st with pleasure thine annoy?*

The first phrase, "music to hear", serves both as an address and as a declaration of the subject of the verse, depending on whom is being addressed. "Music" is interesting both for its clearly understood meaning as well as for referring to its origin, "the art of the muses", and as Hamnet is Shakespeare's muse, Shakespeare is the muse of the sonnets'.

If each sonnet is intended to be sounded out, then the sequence itself becomes one long song, but music is not always enjoyable and in this case Shakespeare's grief is its theme. The sonnet is the music, and "hears" itself only when read out loud or sung by the reader; if it is Shakespeare reading it out loud it becomes a farewell, but if it's the reader then it is both giving life and voice back to Shakespeare as well as a song that mourns him and his son.

The sonnet receives its words from Shakespeare, and is receiving his music whenever he touches pen to paper. It also receives his music when the reader reads the words out loud. The sonnet loves its master, even though it must take on all of his sadness and longing, but it also loves its mistress: a very different kind of love, a grateful love for the reader bringing it back from the darkness behind the cover of the closed book.

Some of the sonnets are filled with love, and some with hate.

The word "annoy" comes from the Old French "to be hateful to", and here it is to be noted that regardless of who the subject and object are in these verses, the relationship is two-way; depending on which side of the sonnet looking glass the subject is on, they may be giving or receiving, happily or hatefully. The sonnet loves Shakespeare even though it receives grief and bitterness along with love; both Shakespeare and the reader love the sonnets in spite of the tragedy embedded in them.

> *If the true concord of well tuned sounds,*
> *By unions married do offend thine ear,*
> *They do but sweetly chide thee, who confounds*
> *In singleness the parts that thou should'st bear:*

The sonnets are well-tuned in every sense of the word, but also in the punning sense of being a song about the well in which Narcissus - Shakespeare - sees his reflection.

"Concord" meant "of one mind" in Old French, originally from the words "together" (con) and "heart" (cord) in Latin. Its use as "agreement", in addition to the harmonious agreement of sounds, recalls for us the term "contracted" from the first sonnet, "married".

"Confounds" both means "to put to shame" and "to mix together, confuse or perplex". "Bear" both means to "carry" or "sustain", and "to give birth".

Ignoring the traditionally understood sexual references, let us focus on the ideas of music and marriage: each sonnet agrees with the others, is married to the others, a theme that's been strongly established since the very first sonnet. They can be offensive or unpleasant to the ear, certainly, in particular because from sonnet 1 they're desperately and harshly instructing Shakespeare, the sonnets themselves and the reader to get to work on their legacy and reminding all the actors of their failings in this regard.

Whoever is being addressed, Shakespeare or the reader, is confounding, or mixing together, the individual sonnets of the sequence. Shakespeare is bearing the sequence by writing it, the reader bears it by reading it.

Additionally, as sonnet 8 is the latest sonnet, it is confounding - shaming or perplexing - the rest of the sequence if it doesn't lead on to more sonnets.

> *Mark how one string sweet husband to an other,*
> *Strikes each in each by mutual ordering;*
> *Resembling sire, and child, and happy mother,*
> *Who, all in one, one pleasing note do sing:*

"Mark" means to take note of, but is also a verb instructing Shakespeare and the sonnet to sign, or indicate, that the ordering of the sequence is critical to producing the correct music. "String" in those days meant the string of an instrument as well as "a number of objects arranged in a line". The word "strikes" recalls the word "offends" from the previous quatrain, and each sonnet, each line or "string", works together with its predecessor and its successor to form a coherent narrative, or pleasing note.

"Resembling", as mentioned in the previous episode, may connote "re-assembling". The sire, child and mother have a double meaning: biologically, they refer to Shakespeare, his son Hamnet and his wife Anne Hathaway; figuratively, they refer to Shakespeare, the sonnet and the reader. The lines and verses of the sonnets represent Shakespeare and his family, recalling his happier days prior to Hamnet's and Shakespeare's deaths, and when consumed as a single body of work they carry the following message:

> *Whose speechless song being many, seeming one,*
> *Sings this to thee thou single wilt prove none.*

The speechless song, already mentioned in my analysis of sonnets 3, 4 and 7, is the written sonnet. "Seeming" meant both "appearing to be" and "befitting"; there are many sonnets that appear to be a unified whole when consumed in sequence, and when read in such a fashion form a complete memory of Shakespeare, but when read individually "prove none" and are insufficient evidence of the Bard's efforts.

"Wilt", from the 1690's, meant "fade, droop, and wither" as it does today, and the rose that is the symbol of the Bard and the metaphor for his sonnet reflections, will wither and fade if the sonnets are not written and read.

The accepted modernised text differs from the original in that "thou single wilt prove none" has been put in quotes to indicate that that is the song being sung, but that prevents us from reading "Sings this: 'to thee, thou single wilt prove none'" which I believe is also valid. In that case, we can even go so far as to group "thou single wilt" into the subject of the sentence, which would suggest that a single "wilt" would prove nothing, whereas many "wilts" would be sufficient to bear witness for the Bard.

This sequence sings one continuous theme - with no legacy, you are nothing: not Shakespeare, not the individual sonnets, and not the reader. Shakespeare is making music with the sonnets, each sonnet being a single note of a beautiful, but tragically sad song that mourns his biological family. That family is long gone, but his metaphorical family, his sonnets and their readers, remain. It is by this reading that we prove that Shakespeare's efforts were - pun intended - not in vain.

SONNET 9

1609 QUARTO VERSION

IS it for feare to wet a widdowes eye,
That thou conſum'ſt thy ſelfe in ſingle life?
Ah;if thou iſſuleſſe ſhalt hap to die,
The world will waile thee like a makeleſſe wife,
The world wilbe thy widdow and ſtill weepe,
That thou no forme of thee haſt left behind ,
When euery priuat widdow well may keepe,
By childrens eyes,her husbands ſhape in minde:
Looke what an vnthrift in the world doth ſpend
Shifts but his place,for ſtill the world inioyes it
But beauties waſte hath in the world an end,
And kept vnvſde the vſer ſo deſtroyes it:
 No loue toward others in that boſome ſits

That on himſelfe ſuch murdrous ſhame commits.

ANALYSIS

Is it for fear to wet a widow's eye,
That thou consum'st thy self in single life?

The word "widow" is historically invested with a lot more meanings than simply "a woman whose husband has died", including "bereft" from Latin and "unmarried man" from Greek. Additionally, from the mid-15th century it meant "woman separated from or deserted by her husband". These meanings are all viable in context: Shakespeare and his wife were both widowed by their son, Shakespeare and his wife most likely became distanced as a result of Hamnet's death - as is normal and understandable - and if each sonnet is its own individual then it will be widowed by Shakespeare's death and is destined to make its readers cry. This last is borne out in "A Lover's Complaint", the attached poem, which describes the reader's experience as follows: "Oft did she heave her napkin to her eyne, / Which on it had conceited characters, / Laund'ring the silken figures in the brine / That seasoned woe had pelleted in tears".

"Consume", from the late 14th century, meant "to destroy by separating into parts which cannot be reunited, as by burning or eating", which ties in strongly to the previously established theme discussing the individual sonnets versus the sequence as a whole, and also references Cupid's fire, which consumed Narcissus.

By the late 16th century, when Shakespeare began writing the sonnets, the second meaning of "consume", "to engage the full attention and energy of", had taken hold.

These opening lines suggest a number of things: Shakespeare producing the sonnets, or Shakespeare not producing the sonnets, the sonnet not leading on to another sonnet; all this to avoid making Shakespeare or his wife cry for their son, or Shakespeare and the sonnets cry for each other, or the reader cry for Shakespeare's and their own perceived loss.

> *Ah! if thou issueless shalt hap to die,*
> *The world will wail thee like a makeless wife,*
> *The world will be thy widow and still weep,*
> *That thou no form of thee hast left behind,*
> *When every private widow well may keep,*
> *By children's eyes, her husband's shape in mind:*

"Make", "form" and "keep" tie these lines together, they're quite straightforward and consistent with all previously established themes; "private" suggests "deprived", "private individual", or "common person".

The eyes are Shakespeare's sonnet reflections, his lost Hamnet's eyes, and the husband to those reflections is Shakespeare. A private widow, in this sense, can be the reader, but we can also read this as each individual sonnet being a private widow of Shakespeare, keeping his image alive in the mind of the reader.

While we can read line 7 as "every private widow may keep well", we can also read "widow well" as a qualified noun, with each sonnet a "widow well" that Shakespeare's reflection has resided in.

> *Look what an unthrift in the world doth spend*
> *Shifts but his place, for still the world enjoys it*
> *But beauty's waste hath in the world an end,*
> *And kept unused the user so destroys it:*

The word "unthrift" appears only three times in the sonnet sequence, in sonnets 4, 9 and 13, and in sonnet 4 we established that Shakespeare is generously spending his words, his very soul, on the sonnet sequence. To "shift" in Middle English didn't mean to move, but did include meanings such as "arrange, place, order, divide, and distribute"; what we're seeing here, in other words, is Shakespeare's soul being divided and arranged into the sequence in order that the world can enjoy it just as it enjoys Shakespeare's physical existence. "Wasting" beauty by putting it into sonnet form has an end, or purpose, and is finite: if the beauty, or Shakespeare's spirit, is not shared or captured in the text then it will be destroyed.

There's another way of looking at this, however: if what is being spent is the reader's time and attention, then readers are putting themselves in Shakespeare's place and letting the Bard take over their minds; failure to read the sonnets is - at least as far as the sonnets are concerned - a destructive act.

No love toward others in that bosom sits
That on himself such murd'rous shame commits.

This is the second time the word "shame" appears, and it is described as "murderous". Not having a son is a murderous shame, and Shakespeare not writing himself and his lost son into the sonnet sequence is a murderous shame.

Finally, and just as murderously shameful, is us not taking the time to read Shakespeare's sonnets.

SONNET 10

1609 QUARTO VERSION

FOr ſhame deny that thou bear'ſt loue to any
Who for thy ſelfe art ſo vnprouident
Graunt if thou wilt,thou art belou'd of many,
But that thou none lou'ſt is moſt euident:
For thou art ſo poſſeſt with murdrous hate,
That gainſt thy ſelfe thou ſtickſt not to conſpire,
Seeking that beautious roofe to ruinate
Which to repaire ſhould be thy chiefe deſire :
O change thy thought,that I may change my minde,
Shall hate be fairer log'd then gentle loue?
Be as thy preſence is gracious and kind,
Or to thy ſelfe at leaſt kind harted proue,
Make thee an other ſelfe for loue of me,

That beauty ſtill may liue in thine or thee.

ANALYSIS

> *For shame deny that thou bear'st love to any*
> *Who for thy self art so unprovident*
> *Grant if thou wilt, thou art beloved of many,*
> *But that thou none lov'st is most evident:*

Sonnet 10 continues in the same vein as its forebears, although here becomes almost accusatory before turning to pleading.

"Provident" meant "foreseeing", or "prudent", so "unprovident" here means blind to the future, or reckless in not preparing sufficiently for it. "Wilt" recalls sonnet 8, where I suggested that it might mean "wilt" in the botanical sense of the wilting of a rose that represents the sonnets.

With those definitions out of the way, the first quatrain appears to be saying that Shakespeare should be ashamed - the same shame that is mentioned on a number of occasions throughout the sequence - for not passing on his predecessors's love and rendering them unprovided for and futureless. In the same way, this selfish sonnet should be ashamed for not producing another sonnet and thereby bringing an end to the sequence.

> *For thou art so possessed with murderous hate,*
> *That 'gainst thy self thou stick'st not to conspire,*
> *Seeking that beauteous roof to ruinate*
> *Which to repair should be thy chief desire.*

Use of the word "stick" has historically been derived from ideas relating to sharp sticks, meaning "pierce", "stab", "transfix", "goad", "to remain embedded, fixed or fastened", and even - from Greek - to be "marked by a pointed instrument"; any of those meanings apply well here, in addition to its Middle English evolution to "remain permanently in mind".

"Conspire" meant to "agree together to commit a criminal or reprehensible act", in Old French literally meaning "to breath together" or even, in line with sonnet 8's singing metaphor, "to blow together".

"Roof" here could mean "roof, ceiling, top, summit; heaven, sky", which is possibly a synecdoche for "house, family, or lineage", but could also refer to the sky over the metaphorical world created by the sonnets.

Shakespeare and his sonnet are accusing each other of being filled with "murderous hate" for not persevering and cooperating in the production of the sonnets, but there's another accusation embedded here which is towards the reader, who murders the spirit of the sequence by not persevering, by not continuing to read the sonnets out loud and for not keeping them in mind.

> *O change thy thought, that I may change my mind,*
> *Shall hate be fairer lodged than gentle love?*
> *Be as thy presence is gracious and kind,*
> *Or to thyself at least kind hearted prove,*

In the accepted modernised text, commas have been inserted into "Be, as they presence is, gracious and kind", but without the commas we can also read "Be, as thy presence is gracious and kind".

The words "change thy thought" usher in a change of tone to one of gentle pleading, and as this is Shakespeare instructing his reflection (and vice versa) the change occurs the very instant it is thought of. Shakespeare and his sonnet reflection appreciate each others' presence, but they are both reliant on the generosity of the reader in lending the sonnets their presence and breath.

> *Make thee an other self for love of me,*
> *That beauty still may live in thine or thee.*

If Shakespeare loves this sonnet then he must produce another sonnet, conversely if this sonnet loves Shakespeare then it will precede another sonnet; as long as there are more sonnets, beauty will have an opportunity to live on in them.

SONNET 11

1609 QUARTO VERSION

AS faſt as thou ſhalt wane ſo faſt thou grow'ſt,
In one of thine,from that which thou departeſt,
And that freſh bloud which yongly thou beſtow'ſt,
Thou maiſt call thine,when thou from youth conuerteſt,
Herein liues wiſdome,beauty,and increaſe,
Without this follie,age,and could decay,
If all were minded ſo,the times ſhould ceaſe,
And threeſcore yeare would make the world away:
Let thoſe whom nature hath not made for ſtore,
Harſh,featureleſſe,and rude , barrenly perriſh,
Looke whom ſhe beſt indow'd,ſhe gaue the more;
Which bountious guift thou ſhouldſt in bounty cherriſh,
She caru'd thee for her ſeale,and ment therby,

Thou ſhouldſt print more,not let that coppy die.

ANALYSIS

As fast as thou shalt wane so fast thou grow'st,
In one of thine, from that which thou departest,
And that fresh blood which youngly thou bestow'st,
Thou mayst call thine, when thou from youth convertest,

In addition to "rapid" and "quickly", in Old English, "fast" meant "firm, fixed, constant, watertight, enclosed, and fortified", and related to the noun "fæsten" meaning "fortress, cloister, enclosure, or prison". This relates to the trenches image from sonnet 2 and sonnet 5's "sap" and "liquid prisoner".

The word "wane" meant to "make or become smaller gradually, diminish, decline, fade", and in addition to its use to describe the phases of the moon it also describes a ship leaving for the horizon as seen from the shore. This is reinforced by the following line's "departest", which recalls the dedication and sonnet 6 where the adventurer - the sonnet sequence - is setting forth on its journey.

I find it interesting that it was only in the early 15th century that the word "wax" was replaced with "grow", and the sense of waxing and waning would have invoked the phases of the moon as that use was already in circulation from the 1300's. This is important, which we'll see when we get to the following quatrain.

As I discussed when analysing sonnets 1 and 2, ink is the blood of the sonnets. The sonnets are written to capture Shakespeare's youth, and so it is the fresh blood of the poet that fuels them; Shakespeare can still call the sonnet's ink "his" when he is old. Likewise, the fresh sonnets take ink away from the older ones, but still belong to their predecessors that they share the sequence with.

To "convert" might have meant "a change or turn from one religion to another", but I'm quite confident that the intention here is "to change into another form or substance," or "transmute".

Shakespeare's youth is being converted into sonnets, where it will remain youthful forever.

> *Herein lives wisdom, beauty, and increase,*
> *Without this folly, age, and could decay,*
> *If all were minded so, the times should cease,*
> *And threescore year would make the world away:*

"Folly" comes from French, meaning "madness", or "stupidity". "Herein" contrasts with "without", so wisdom, beauty and increase - and legacy - live in the sonnet sequence whereas folly, age and cold decay continue outside of it. At the same time, the sonnets are able to live "without" the foolish madness of ageing and decaying.

The accepted modernisation of "could decay" is "cold decay", which is interesting because the original fits better with the "should" in the following line. I suspect that while "cold decay" does seem to work, the intention here is rather "possibility of decay".

"Minded" means "remembered", "perceived", "to give heed to", as well as "be of the same mind", and "heed" in Old English meant "observe; to take care, attend, care for, protect, take charge of".

If everyone were remembered like Shakespeare in his sonnets by being converted into poetry, or if all his sonnets were remembered, then all divisions of time would become irrelevant to the everliving poetry that is represented by the rose's distillation discussed in sonnet 5.

"Threescore year" refers to the age Shakespeare might have hoped to live, and might be related to the biblical "threescore and ten", but numbers and the passage of time are central to the sonnet sequence and it's far more likely that this is a reference to sonnet 60, which runs parallel to sonnet 11 in a number of interesting ways. The relationship of the lunar phase in sonnet 11 to the tides in sonnet 60 was well-established long before

Shakespeare's time so it's no surprise that he would use it to connect these two sonnets, especially in conjunction with the nautical sense of the word "departure" from the first quatrain that's qualified by "would make the world away", where "away" originally meant "from one's place" or "from one's possession", and in the 16th century acquired the additional meaning of "onward in time". This reminds us of the dedication, and foreshadows the words "bark" (ship) and "boat" in sonnets 80 and 116; the sonnet sequence is the ship that sails the seas of eternity, carrying its sonnet passengers to the reader.

> *Let those whom nature hath not made for store,*
> *Harsh, featureless, and rude, barrenly perish,*
> *Look whom she best endowed, she gave the more;*
> *Which bounteous gift thou shouldst in bounty cherish,*

"Store" links to sonnet 2's "treasure". "Harsh, featureless and rude" are all very negative, and contrast with the beauty that Shakespeare is inscribing into the sequence. Shakespeare is expressing his right and intention to leave offensive or boring aspects of his character out of the sonnet sequence, to let them die along with his physical body so that his legacy can be free of blemishes.

Endowed meant "provided an income", in particular a "marriage portion", recalling the marriage contract from sonnet 1, and "she gave the more" operates with "bounteous gift" and "bounty" to remind us of sonnet 4's discussion on usury and increasing wealth in order to pass it along to one's heirs.

"Cherish", from the Old French "cher", carried today's meanings of "hold as dear, treat with tenderness and affection" as well as the implicit "expensive".

> *She carved thee for her seal, and meant thereby,*
> *Thou shouldst print more, not let that copy die.*

"Carve" meant "to cut", but also originally "to write into stone". "Seal" comes from the Old French meaning the "seal on a letter", which in turn derives from the latin word "sigillum", which also meant "small picture, engraved figure".

The word "seal" is interesting because the image in the seal is a reflection, a reversed copy of the "sigil", stamp or signet ring, and here each sonnet is being compared directly to the image that Shakespeare has stamped onto it. Moreover, Shakespeare is writing the sonnets to act as his seal, and it is their imprint in the reader's mind that serves as a copy: the sonnets must continue to imprint themselves in more readers, or the original copies will die.

SONNET 12

1609 QUARTO VERSION

WHen I doe count the clock that tels the time,
And ſee the braue day ſunck in hidious night,
When I behold the violet paſt prime,
And ſable curls or ſiluer'd ore with white :
When lofty trees I ſee barren of leaues,
Which erſt from heat did canopie the herd
And Sommers greene all girded vp in ſheaues
Borne on the beare with white and briſtly beard:
Then of thy beauty do I queſtion make
That thou among the waſtes of time muſt goe,
Since ſweets and beauties do them-ſelues forſake,
And die as faſt as they ſee others grow,
And nothing gainſt Times ſieth can make defence

Saue breed to braue him, when he takes thee hence.

ANALYSIS

When I do count the clock that tells the time,
And see the brave day sunk in hideous night,
When I behold the violet past prime,
And sable curls or silvered ore with white:

Time and Death are wonderfully conflated throughout the sonnet sequence, beginning as early as the first sonnet: Time is the Roman god Saturnus, conflated in Ovid's Metamophoses with Chronos, and even today Father Time's scythe is easily recognisable as the implement of the Grim Reaper. Saturn is the god of generation, dissolution, plenty, wealth, agriculture, periodic renewal and liberation, all aspects that are explicitly discussed in Shakespeare's Sonnets.

The word "clock" in Middle English was geared towards the idea of bells and chiming, as well, apparently, as the ornament pattern on a stocking.

Sonnet 12 is a clock that tells the time, suggesting that the first twelve sonnets are hours on a clock and explicitly adding a sense of time to the sonnet reading. It informs us that it is now midnight, a time of death and darkness. Just as the sonnet sequence is a mirror with two sides, so is the sonnet clock a reflection; when the sonnet is read, it tells of a particular time, but from the sonnet's perspective it is the face that reads it that tells the time and gives a sense of its passage: in words, in wrinkles, and in the number of different faces encountered. As has been mentioned before, when the sonnets are not being read they are enshrouded in the darkness of the closed book and remain in timeless stasis that would be experienced as eternity.

In sonnet 11 we read a connection to sonnet 60 with "threescore", but sonnet 12 relates to sonnet 60 as well with there being 60 minutes in an hour. The second line of sonnet 60, "our minutes hasten to their end", ties in neatly with the above analysis.

The adjectives "brave" and "hideous" are words that sent me off on a hunt through Golding's translation of Ovid's Metamorphoses, they're very particular terms and don't appear to be used here in their modern senses: brave already meant "exhibiting courage or courageous endurance" from Middle French's "splendid", or "valiant", but "hideous" meant "terrifying, horrible, or dreadful". In Metamorphoses, the word "brave" is generally used as "splendid" or "courageous", but twice describes particular leaves as "evergreen" and "enduring". The word "hideous", by contrast, generally refers to frightening storms, to awful noises that characters make when they face unimaginable horror, and to the dragon serpent Python that Phoebus slew, which may prove significant as Phoebus has been an established actor in the sequence since sonnet 7.

I find the decision to change "or silvered ore" to "all silvered over" in the accepted modernised text distasteful, and there is no good reason that the violet, curls and ore of lines 3 and 4 cannot be read as three different alternatives.

When lofty trees I see barren of leaves,
Which erst from heat did canopy the herd
And Summer's green all girded up in sheaves
Borne on the bier with white and bristly beard:

"Herd" meant both a quantity of domestic animals, playing into the conceit of livestock and agriculture from the beginning of the sequence, and "a keeping, care, or custody". It is also the noun for the keeper of the herd, as in "shepherd". The sonnet sequence is a store of Shakespeare's creations, referenced as "treasure" since sonnet 2, and serves as their custodian; each sonnet protects an aspect of the Bard, so the covers of the bound volume and each individual page form a canopy that protects and shelters these reflections.

There's an additional pun here, too, with "the herd" being the collection of sonnets that are read aloud, rendered them "heard", and the voice that they lend to their creator, Shakespeare, who is heard through them.

"Summer's green" does not have a possessive apostrophe in the original text, which allows for a reading wherein multiple green summers are girded up.

"To gather up in sheaves" is an expression that appears to have emerged from the 1570s, with sheaves being "grooved wheels to receive cords or pulleys", and bier meaning a "wooden frame on which to carry a load", and a "framework on which a coffin or corpse is laid before burial". The original text has "beare" as opposed to "bier", which suggests "possessing an attribute", "sustaining without sinking", "carry" as well as the act of producing. It also produces an internal rhyme with "beard", visually as well as aurally.

This quatrain is enveloped in an air of pessimism: the trees are not evergreen, the pages of Shakespeare's poetry, grooved with his pen, are bound and scheduled for burial, or at least to be carried in this coffin of a sequence to readings wherein they will be buried again, and this at the same time that Shakespeare himself is ageing, losing the hair that before protected his crown and the thoughts herded beneath it, preparing to be carried to his wintery grave both in real life and as the protagonist in the story of the sequence. At the same time, the sonnets must carry their load and persevere on the winter mission they were created for.

> *Then of thy beauty do I question make*
> *That thou among the wastes of time must go,*
> *Since sweets and beauties do them-selves forsake,*
> *And die as fast as they see others grow,*

The word "question" is quite loaded, its simplified use in today's speech does not account for its history which included a "philosophical or theological problem", an "utterance meant to elicit an answer or discussion", "torture" and "a seeking". It is the last meaning that I find most apt in this context, as Shakespeare has turned his inner "beauty" into sonnets that must venture into the wastes of time while he wastes away without a son to replace him; the sonnets are different from humans in that they do not die as fast as they see others grow, but remain static throughout their journey into eternity.

That Shakespeare is forsaking himself by failing to replace himself with a son is the truth of one side of the sonnet looking glass, on the other we find the sonnets forsaking their creator as they go on their separate adventure.

> *And nothing 'gainst Time's scythe can make defence*
> *Save breed to brave him, when he takes thee hence.*

It seems strange to me in the accepted modernised text the comma after "to brave him" has been moved forward to "save breed, to brave him".

By the end of the 16th century, the word stroke meant both "the mark of a pen" and the striking of a clock; in this sonnet's closing couplet, Time's scythe strikes with each hour that passes, Shakespeare's only son is dead, and his only defence remains in the stroke of his quill.

SONNET 13

1609 QUARTO VERSION

OThat you were your ſelfe,but loue you are
No longer yours,then you your ſelfe here liue,
Againſt this cumming end you ſhould prepare,
And your ſweet ſemblance to ſome other giue.
So ſhould that beauty which you hold in leaſe
Find no determination,then you were
You ſelfe again after your ſelfes deceaſe,
When your ſweet iſſue your ſweet forme ſhould beare.
Who lets ſo faire a houſe fall to decay,
Which husbandry in honour might vphold,
Againſt the ſtormy guſts of winters day
And barren rage of deaths eternall cold?
O none but vnthrifts,deare my loue you know,

You had a Father,let your Son ſay ſo.

ANALYSIS

> *O! That you were your self, but love you are*
> *No longer yours, then you your self here live,*
> *Against this coming end you should prepare,*
> *And your sweet semblance to some other give.*

From the perspective of the sonnet side of the looking glass, the sonnet is speaking both to Shakespeare and to the reader. as aspects of Shakespeare's spirit are being transmuted into the words of the sonnet, they no longer belong to him alone, just as he himself does not get to live in the sonnet but must die a natural death while his copies continue on their adventure.

While the reader's attention is focused on reading the sonnet, they give themselves over to it and, in their imaginations only, live in the world that the sonnet creates. When the writing of this sonnet comes to an end, Shakespeare must lend his spirit to another sonnet, and when the reading comes to an end, the reader must continue on to the next one.

From our side of the looking glass, the sonnet's "self" is Shakespeare but that "self" does not belong to it; the sonnet exists only in the minds of the author and the reader. The sonnet must prepare for the eventuality that it will be completed by the author or reader, and must move on to search for another "sweet semblance". This is reinforced in the word "semblance", which suggests an "imitation" of the Bard, which is a sonnet.

> *So should that beauty which you hold in lease*
> *Find no determination, then you were*
> *You self again after your self's decease,*
> *When your sweet issue your sweet form should bear.*

The word "lease" follows the established theme of legal tender and contracts, with a connotation of "temporary"; "temporary", in context of the sonnet sequence, is the state of the biological author, the reader, and the ephemeral reading experience.

"Determination" in Shakespeare's day meant decision, "a sentence in a suit at law", and the end of a lease; in this context we can reword "so should that beauty which you hold in lease find no determination" as "let us hope that this contract with beauty does not come to an end".

In the accepted modernised text, "You self again" has been changed to "yourself again". While this modification does make sense when following on from the previous line, it prevents us from reading "self" as a verb, in which case this line would read "You exist as your self again after your self is deceased".

The first two lines of this quatrain speak to all three actors: for Shakespeare, his beauty that is "borrowed" from nature is loaned to the sonnet sequence, for the sonnets, it is the Bard's borrowed beauty that is loaned to the reader, and for the reader, the beauty of the sonnets rents space in the reader's mind. In this way, Shakespeare can continue to be himself, repeatedly, even after his body has died.

"Issue" had a few meanings in Shakespeare's day, including "an exit", or "leaving", a "discharge of fluid from the body", "offspring" or "children", "an outcome of an action or a consequence", and, legally, the "end or result of pleadings in a suit" implying "a point of contention between two parties".

The last line of this quatrain can be plainly read as "when your sonnets carry your form", but as the quatrain has already established a legal theme, it seems reasonable to suggest that the sweet issue may refer to the contention between the sonnets' love for Shakespeare, their duty to be discharged, and their relationship with the reader; or, more simply, the argument that the sonnet makes on Shakespeare's behalf. As the word "beare" connects this to the previous sonnet, this has the added effect of loading the expression with the previous sonnet's imagery.

Who lets so fair a house fall to decay,
Which husbandry in honour might uphold,

> *Against the stormy gusts of winter's day*
> *And barren rage of death's eternal cold?*

Husbandry, referred to a few times earlier in the sequence, meant farm management, but it originally meant "management of a household" which here seems more appropriate in addition to the pun on "being a good husband" and having children.

The phrase "barren rage" can be read with barren as an adjective describing empty or unproductive rage, either about death's eternal cold or by death's eternal cold, or as a noun, in which case it would be a barren person who rages about death's eternal cold.

Shakespeare had already let his house fall to decay, to his shame, even if whatever had taken Hamnet's life was outside of his control. This quatrain is self-reflective, but if the output of his "rage" was the sonnet sequence then it was anything but barren. At the same time, this quatrain attempts to motivate the sonnets to uphold Shakespeare's honour to protect the Bard from a more final death.

> *O! none but unthrifts, dear my love you know,*
> *You had a Father, let your Son say so.*

As mentioned before, the word "unthrift" only appears three times in the sonnet sequence, in sonnets 4, 9 and 13. I find it intriguing that the number 4 is 2^2, 9 is 3^2, and 13 is 4 + 9, which if we were dealing with mathematics and triangles would relate sonnet 13 to the hypotenuse of a right-angled triangle.

If we look for the word "thrift" as well as "unthrift", sonnet 2 is included. The word "thrive" may also be connected, because in addition to the meaning we're familiar with today it's strongly related to the word "thrift". The word "thrive" is only found in sonnets 14, 80 and 125, the last two numbers being 4 x 20 and 5 x 25 respectively, so it may well be worth examining this subsequence of sonnets for a thematic relationship even if the math for sonnet 14 doesn't seem to fit.

In the original text, "dear my love you know" is not punctuated, which allows us to read "dear my love, you know" but also "dear, my love you know". I believe the capitalisation of "Father" and "Son" here is significant, quite possibly a religious reference.

As a father, there's something I find particularly heart-wrenching in the final verse of sonnet 13. The sonnets serve Shakespeare in place of his lost son, and one must bear in mind that this line was written by a grieving father to his son's memory. "You had a father", then, takes on a powerful new meaning:

You had a father, Hamnet. Let your sonnet say so.

SONNET 14

1609 QUARTO VERSION

NOt from the ſtars do I my iudgement plucke,
And yet me thinkes I haue Aſtronomy,
But not to tell of good,or euil lucke,
Of plagues,of dearths,or ſeaſons quallity,
Nor can I fortune to breefe my nuits tell;
Pointing to each his thunder, raine and winde,
Or ſay with Princes if it ſhal go wel
By oft predict that I in heauen finde.
But from thine eies my knowledge I deriue,
And conſtant ſtars in them I read ſuch art
As truth and beautie ſhal together thriue
If from thy ſelfe,to ſtore thou wouldſt conuert:
Or elſe of thee this I prognoſticate,

Thy end is Truthes and Beauties doome and date.

ANALYSIS

> *Not from the stars do I my judgement pluck,*
> *And yet me thinks I have Astronomy,*
> *But not to tell of good, or evil luck,*
> *Of plagues, of dearths, or seasons' quality,*

As discussed in the introduction, whenever we read about "stars" it's generally a reference to the eyes of Narcissus' reflection in Ovid's Metamorphoses; in this sonnet, however, the stars serve as both the reflection's eyes and the stars in the sky that astrologers read. Astronomy, in Shakespeare's time, described what we refer to as astrology today.

The word "judgement" follows the previously established legal theme, but brings in the biblical element of The Last Judgement. This is confirmed in the closing couplet's reference to "doom and date".

I find it interesting that the expression "to pluck up" carried the meaning of to "summon up" from as early as the 14th century, which is what we do to Shakespeare's spirit whenever we engage with the sonnets, and I'm fairly confident that it also references the plucking of a string in line with musical theme established in sonnet 8.

In the accepted modernised text "me thinks" is combined to "methinks", but I believe there's an intentional distinction here between "me" and "I".

Putting that all together, this opening quatrain becomes quite dense. Shakespeare is plucking his judgement from the fates, and the sonnets pluck their judgement from their creator. Both are telling each other, and the reader, about themselves and their fortune, but not in the simple whims and conceits that astrologers are known to pander to.

> *Nor can I fortune to brief minutes tell;*
> *Pointing to each his thunder, rain and wind,*

> *Or say with Princes if it shall go well*
> *By oft predict that I in heaven find.*

The second quatrain reinforces the first's conceit. The word "minutes" is used here in context of astronomy, which relates to sonnet 60's waves and the established nautical theme, suggesting that what Shakespeare is doing with his sonnets is attempting to navigate the seas of time by the stars, or reflected eyes, of the reader.

While I'm sure there's plenty more interesting material in there, I don't believe it would significantly alter this interpretation of the sonnet. I wouldn't be surprised to learn that it contained some interesting numerical references, too, but as it is the first appearance of the word "thunder" in the first book of Golding's translation of Ovid's Metamorphoses is in line 62, which is preceded by the line "There hath he placed mist and cloudes, and for to feare mens mindes, / The thunder and the lightning eke, with colde and blustring windes".

The next interesting mention of thunder accompanies the lightning that Zeus sent down to destroy Phaethon, Phoebus' prince, who has already been referenced in sonnet 7 and whose father warned him not to drive the sun's chariot through the heavens. I suspect this is not a coincidence.

Another interesting note, connecting this sonnet to sonnet 18, is that as the sonnets are intended to be read aloud, and "I in heaven" can be read "eye in heaven" which opens that line up to some additional interpretations.

> *But from thine eyes my knowledge I derive,*
> *And constant stars in them I read such art*
> *As truth and beauty shall together thrive*
> *If from thy self, to store thou wouldst convert:*

The word derive is a peculiar choice, coming from the Old French "to flow, pour out, originate", and in 16th century English it evolved from "obtain by a process of reasoning" to include "arise by a process of word-formation".

As discussed in the previous sonnet's analysis, the word "thrive" presents an intriguing numerical connection.

As we've seen many times before, many of the sonnet lines can be read in a variety of ways based on where the emphasis is placed; if we read line 9 as "but from thine eyes MY knowledge I derive", we can hear Shakespeare deriving his own knowledge back from the sonnets, literally reading his own words back to himself. In the accepted modernised text, "And constants stars in them I read such art" has been separated by commas in a way that prevents seeing that the constant stars could be in "thine eyes".

The more straightforward reading of that is that the sonnets are deriving their knowledge from Shakespeare: in the constant, fixed, invariable, sonnet windows into Shakespeare's soul, we find truth and beauty together as they have been converted from the original - biological - Bard.

This conceit also works when speaking to the reader, albeit in a much more roundabout manner. Metaphorically, the sonnet can read the reader's eyes to see what kind of store they will provide for Shakespeare's words, and literally, perhaps the sonnet "reads" its own words being reflected in the reader's eyes.

Or else of thee this I prognosticate,

Thy end is Truth's and Beauty's doom and date.

The closing couplet has two significant changes in the accepted modernised text. The first being that the comma at the end of line 13 has been replaced with a colon, directing the reader to read line 14 as the prediction when "this" could well refer to the sonnet in its entirety. The second is that the capitalisation of "Truth" and "Beauty" has been ignored and they've been transcribed in the singular as opposed to plural. While I've left the latter in because I don't think it's wrong *per se*, it must be noted that "Truths and Beauties" is quite possibly more correct and suggests that they refer to the many sonnets.

Shakespeare is plucking his doom from the hands of fate by writing his spirit into the sonnet sequence, which is summoned by the constant stars, the faithful reader's eyes who continue to read the sonnets. The sonnets tell the future - in that they tell the future reader - of the Bard's youth, of his love, his loss, his truth and his beauty.

When the reader reaches the end of the sonnet sequence, they will close the book on Shakespeare's truth and beauty and return the sonnets to their doom of eternal darkness.

However, if the sonnets were really to come to an end, if they were destroyed, or lost, or simply forgotten, that would be the end of Shakespeare's legacy, the Bard's final death, our everliving poet's doom.

SONNET 15

1609 QUARTO VERSION

WHen I confider euery thing that growes
Holds in perfection but a little moment.
That this huge ftage prefenteth nought but fhowes
Whereon the Stars in fecret influence comment.
When I perceiue that men as plants increafe,
Cheared and checkt euen by the felfe-fame skie:
Vaunt in their youthfull fap, at height decreafe,
And were their braue ftate out of memory.
Then the conceit of this inconftant ftay,
Sets you moft rich in youth before my fight,
Where waftfull time debateth with decay
To change your day of youth to fullied night,
And all in war with Time for loue of you

As he takes from you, I ingraft you new.

ANALYSIS

> *When I consider every thing that grows*
> *Holds in perfection but a little moment.*
> *That this huge stage presenteth nought but shows*
> *Whereon the Stars in secret influence comment.*

"Consider" is a heavily loaded term; while its modern meaning has been in use since the 14th century, it includes a suggestion of "to observe the stars" from Latin, and from the 1530's "to regard in a particular light". In combination with the "stars" of line 4 we see that this opening verse continues the astronomy (or astrology) metaphor from the previous sonnet. It is interesting that this is the first time the word "Stars" has been capitalised, and I suspect that its significance is in referring to the reader's eyes.

Just like living things capture perfection for just a tiny moment in time, the sonnets capture only a tiny moment of Shakespeare's perfection. The world is a stage, certainly, but so is the sonnet sequence, and the shows are presented by the sonnets to the reader whose "comment" - a word strongly linked to the word "consider" - are as inaccessible to the sonnets as the original thoughts of their author. Additionally, each meeting of the sonnets with the reader is a secret from Shakespeare, where "secret" meant "concealed" and "apart", as is the Bard's influence on the reader through his words.

As I've mentioned before, Shakespeare is using his sonnets to possess the reader for the duration of the spell, influencing them to speak his words out loud in order to keep them, and thereby himself, alive.

> *When I perceive that men as plants increase,*
> *Cheered and checked even by the self-same sky:*
> *Vaunt in their youthful sap, at height decrease,*
> *And wear their brave state out of memory.*

Men and plants are here described as being equivalent, and

plants or leaves, as we've seen in earlier sonnets, appear to be metaphors for the pages containing the sonnets. The youthful sap is the ink that pours from Shakespeare's veins, and each sonnet's reading is a sonnet's day: when the reader's eyes reach the middle of the page they begin to descend towards the end, and once the reader reaches the end and begins the next one the previous one is worn out of memory.

In the original text, the word "wear" is spelled "were", which produces an ambiguity in the remainder of the line: the men, or sonnets, lived "their brave state" or even "their brave words" outside the limits of what will be remembered going forward.

> *Then the conceit of this inconstant stay,*
> *Sets you most rich in youth before my sight,*
> *Where wasteful time debateth with decay*
> *To change your day of youth to sullied night,*

"Conceit" meant both "a thought, notion, something formed in the mind" and in Shakespeare's day would already have suggested vanity which plays into the overarching theme of Narcissus and Echo.

"Stay" has a few meanings, one of which recalls the nautical adventure theme and one which means "a piece of wood used as a support", which neatly falls into the previous quatrain's plant theme.

It fascinates me that while lots of the original text's capitalisations have been ignored in the accepted modernised text, line 11's "time" was capitalised. I admit that it's difficult to not read it capitalised, but I believe that this was an intentional choice.

Spoken from the sonnet to Shakespeare, the sonnet sequence makes the author rich in youth "before my sight", meaning both in the sonnet's eyes, as a precursor to the sonnet being read by the reader, and as the sonnet in front of the reader's eyes.

Spoken from Shakespeare to the sonnet, Shakespeare sees the

sonnet as rich in his own youth, and the "you" that is the sonnet is, in the printing press, "set" in a state of rich youth.

"Wasteful time" is set in opposition to decay: Shakespeare and the reader must choose between wasting their time on the sonnets and letting Shakespeare's memory decay.

> *And all in war with Time for love of you*
> *As he takes from you, I engraft you new.*

The closing couplet of sonnet 15 elegantly brings the sonnet's conceits together: "all" refers to all the sonnets of the sequence as well as to all of Shakespeare's "wasteful" efforts to write them. Shakespeare, the sonnets and the reader all battle with Father Time to preserve the Bard's memory and legacy. While Shakespeare grafts a new sonnet to the sequence even as he completes the previous one, the sonnets and the reader graft youth to the Bard's memory even as Time strips it or takes it further away from him.

SONNET 16

1609 QUARTO VERSION

BVt wherefore do not you a mightier waie
Make warre vppon this bloudie tirant time?
And fortifie your felfe in your decay
With meanes more bleffed then my barren rime?
Now ftand you on the top of happie houres,
And many maiden gardens yet vnfet,
With vertuous wifh would beare your liuing flowers,
Much liker then your painted counterfeit:
So fhould the lines of life that life repaire
Which this (Times penfel or my pupill pen)
Neither in inward worth nor outward faire
Can make you liue your felfe in eies of men,
To giue away your felfe, keeps your felfe ftill,

And you muft liue drawne by your owne fweet fkill,

ANALYSIS

> *But wherefore do not you a mightier way*
> *Make war upon this bloody tyrant time?*
> *And fortify your self in your decay*
> *With means more blessed then my barren rhyme?*

We can summarise the opening quatrain in modern English as "But why don't you fight inexorable time with something more blessed than my rhyme?". As usual, this can be read in both directions, between Shakespeare and his sonnet reflection between the sonnet and the reader.

Here it is useful to recall that the reader is expected to adopt the role of Echo in the sequence, and as a reader consciously reading this sonnet out loud and addressing the sonnet reflexively, sonnet 16 is an excellent example of how well this works. The reader is not a poet, and so the reader's repetition of the sonnet's rhymes are "barren" and we can read this quatrain as the reader asking the sonnet why it doesn't fortify itself with stronger defences than the reader's empty words.

While the modernised "means more blessed than my barren rhyme" makes sense, the original text's "then" allows for the possibility that the barren rhyme is preceded by the "means more blessed", likely alluding to Shakespeare's biological children.

> *Now stand you on the top of happy hours,*
> *And many maiden gardens yet unset,*
> *With virtuous wish would bear your living flowers,*
> *Much liker then your painted counterfeit:*

"Now stand you" can be read both as a passive description of a current state, or as an instruction.

As a passive description, this quatrain is stating that the sonnet has many happy hours of reading ahead of it, and at only 16 sonnets there are many blank pages yet to fill; blank pages with a virtuous wish to carry Shakespeare's embedded spirits to the reader to breathe them new life, which would be more like the biological Shakespeare than the counterfeit sonnets could ever hope to be. Alternatively, that last line could simply mean "more likeable than this sonnet in particular".

As an instruction, Shakespeare, the sonnet and the reader are being instructed to get to work with their writing and reading.

Some have suggested that "liker" is understood to mean "more like", and that "then" is to be read as "than", but I'm not convinced. If Shakespeare is speaking to himself through the sonnet, this last line could also be saying that the Bard's painted counterfeit, the sonnet, would be more liked once it has succeeded in planting his words in the ensuing empty pages and the mind of the reader.

> *So should the lines of life that life repair*
> *Which this (Times pencil or my pupil pen)*
> *Neither in inward worth nor outward fair*
> *Can make you live your self in eyes of men,*

"Repair" means both "to mend" and "to go" in the sense of "to go to a place", and Shakespeare is mending his broken legacy by embedding his life in the lines of the sonnet.

"Pencil" meant a "painter's brush", which could be used as a verb meaning to mark or sketch using that implement. "Pupil" meant "orphan child, disciple or student" as well as "centre of the eye". The sonnets are the orphan children of Shakespeare, as well as his disciples, and they are also his eyes (which, according to sonnet 24, serve as the windows to his soul). "Pen" is both a writing implement and an "enclosure for animals", as well as the verbs for putting something in writing and for putting an animal in an enclosure. The latter meaning is in line with the established farming theme.

With these meanings the text in parentheses, "Times pencil or my pupil pen" can be unpacked to "Father Time's creation and creator, or Shakespeare's orphaned disciple and writer, or entrapped orphaned disciple".

"Outward fair" might mean beauty, or fairness, but I believe it's possible readings were intending to include the identically spelled french "faire", meaning "to do or make", as well as "fare", meaning a journey, a payment for passage, and a person conveyed in a vehicle.

Let's put all that into a reading, temporarily disregarding the parenthesis: "The lines of words that embody and remake Shakespeare's spirit / should follow the previous instructions to beget more sonnets / which this poet, or sonnet, or reader / can make you live as your self in men's eyes / neither in inner worth nor outward passage".

Rewording the quatrain in this manner highlights the problematic nature of the words "which this... neither... can make..."; it is natural to derive "which this sonnet cannot make you live" from the positioning of the word "neither" in the middle, but it is also possible to read from this that the sonnet *can* make you live as your self in men's eyes, but not without losing the true depth of character or appearance of the original author.

With the parenthesis reinstated, then, either this poet, or sonnet, or reader is playing the role of both Father Time's paintbrush and Shakespeare's writing disciple, or they are being manipulated by those entities.

An alternate interpretation of the parentheses is that they produce a space to indicate that the sonnet is addressing Shakespeare, who is the painter's brush used by Father Time, or the sonnet, who is his eye, and will become his orphan child.

> *To give away your self, keeps yourself still,*
> *And you must live drawn by your own sweet skill.*

The closing couplet reminds us of the lending theme established back in sonnet 4, and the word "still" is interesting because it has the natural meaning of "even now" or "yet", but also the additional meanings of "motionless" and "quiet", which describe the fixed and voiceless sonnet text.

To maintain his self and his legacy, Shakespeare must give himself away in the form of the sonnets. He must live on in the lines that he has written with his own sweet skill.

SONNET 17

1609 QUARTO VERSION

WHo will beleeue my verſe in time to come,
If it were fild with your moſt high deſerts?
Though yet heauen knowes it is but as a tombe
Which hides your life , and ſhewes not halfe your parts:
If I could write the beauty of your eyes,
And in freſh numbers number all your graces,
The age to come would ſay this Poet lies,
Such heauenly touches nere toucht earthly faces.
So ſhould my papers (yellowed with their age)
Be ſcorn d,like old men of leſſe truth then tongue,
And your true rights be termed a Poets rage,
And ſtretched miter of an Antique ſong.
But were ſome childe of yours aliue that time,
You ſhould liue twiſe in it,and in my rime.

ANALYSIS

Sonnet 17 is one of the more straightforward sonnets, wherein Shakespeare speaks to himself through the verse. It is possible to stretch the intention to the reader as well, but I'm going to focus on the dialogue between Shakespeare and the sonnets.

> *Who will believe my verse in time to come,*
> *If it were filled with your most high deserts?*
> *Though yet heaven knows it is but as a tomb*
> *Which hides your life, and shows not half your parts:*

"Deserts" is a loaded word, as it incorporates the modern meanings of "waterless" and "barren", as he's referred to his rhyme in previous sonnets, but also the meaning that we now only remember in the phrase "just deserts", which is "something that is deserved or merited". Other, older meanings of "merit" and "recompense" tie in with the lending theme established in sonnet 4, and to "leave" or "abandon", which is still in use today.

With all of the above, we can see that the sonnets are filled with barren verse, with the poet's merits, with compensation for his efforts, and with his spirit that has abandoned his biological body.

This is the third time we've seen the word "tomb", or fourth if we include the word "grave", though this is the first time we're seeing it used positively: the sonnet sequence is the tomb which secretly contains Shakespeare's spirit.

With respect to the numerical play I discussed when analysing sonnets 11 through 14, "half your parts" has brought me to take a look at sonnet 77, the exact middle of the 154 sonnets and what **shakespeares-sonnets.com** calls a "climacteric", for which I quote: "All the sonnets bearing the climacteric numbers, which are multiples of seven or nine, show evidence of being placed purposively. They usually interrupt a set or sequence which has some unifying theme, as here, where the sequence runs from 76 to 86, apart from the interruptions of the climacteric numbers 77 and 81. The precise significance of the use of these numbers in the sonnets is unknown, although it is clear that the sonnets set at these crucial points were carefully chosen, and that their position is not the result of any accidental placing."

Sonnet 77 just so happens to be a sonnet that summarises a lot of the established themes. In brief: the sonnet reflects the ageing of the poet, the sonnets marking the time invested in them, the blank pages being imprinted with Shakespeare's mind, mouthed graves (whether the sonnets or the minds of the readers) remembering Shakespeare, Shakespeare's "brain children" delivered and committed to the "wasteful" pages, the Bard making a new "mind acquaintance" of both the sonnet and the reader, and these qualities all enriching the sonnet sequence and profiting Shakespeare with a valuable and enduring legacy.

"Shows not half your parts" is even more interesting, as show (or "shewe", as it was pronounced then) meant to "let be seen", "put in sight", and "make known", in particular to make available for examination; but also the act of exhibiting, a "display" or "spectacle", and "an appearance put on with the intention to deceive". This last meaning is particularly appropriate when considered within the context of a sonnet that discusses Shakespeare employing deception by downplaying his qualities in order to maintain credulity in ages to come.

It must also be noted that the expression "shows not half your parts" is a reference to the "blason", the poetic technique of praising a woman by separating her body into its constituent parts for individual praise, as well as the description of a coat of arms, or the coat of arms itself, from which the poetic form derives its name. As discussed in the introduction, the coat of arms was of particular significance to Shakespeare, but regarding the poetic technique this verse functions as both a description of what Shakespeare has reflexively done to himself with the sonnets while simultaneously making a disparaging remark about this technique which was in popular use in sonnet writing.

This might be a good time to mention that there is delicious irony in the fact that Shakespeare's only published work, arguably the most important of all his creations, is in the form of sonnets which is a poetic form that he continually poked fun at through his plays. Not only were his characters' attempts at writing sonnets pathetic and used for comedic effect, but he would make a point of showing that only women read sonnets and that they weren't to be taken seriously as an art form. This is, in my opinion, what makes the attached poem "A Lover's Complaint" so elegant: it's a poem about a woman who has read Shakespeare's sonnets and been convinced that she alone was being addressed as their intended lover, when in fact they are exclusively faithful to their creator while sharing with anyone who would read them their, and I quote, "thousand favours", "amber, crystal, and ... beaded jet", "folded schedules", "many a ring of posied gold and bone", "letters sadly penn'd in blood", "With sleided silk feat and affectedly Enswathed, and seal'd to curious secrecy".

> *If I could write the beauty of your eyes,*
> *And in fresh numbers number all your graces,*
> *The age to come would say this Poet lies,*
> *Such heavenly touches ne'er touched earthly faces.*

"Graces" contrasts with "deserts", as they are unmerited favours from God, and "divine grace" refers us back to the idea of pardon, and excuse, which follows the established legal theme.

The "fresh numbers" are the freshly written sonnets, and "number all your graces" continues the theme of the blason.

According to **shakespeares-sonnets.com**, "Verses were sometimes referred to as numbers because of their musical quality, and the fact that one could count the number of stresses to a line". "Poet" in Shakespeare's day meant both "poet" as we know it today as well as "singer", in line with the musical theme established since sonnet 8; this is followed by the word "heavenly", which apparently was often used with reference to "music of the spheres".

The accepted reading of the word "nere" as "never", for "such heavenly touches never touched earthly faces", is clearly the reasonable interpretation, but because the original is written with no punctuation and the spelling is "nere" I suspect that its intention is ambiguous, and that it could also be read as "near". That would shift the reading of this quatrain from "if I could capture your beauty and graces in these pages then people would say that I'm lying and that nothing of the sort existed" to "if I could capture your beauty and graces in these pages then people would say that I'm dead and that such heavenly touch nearly touched the readers' earthly faces".

So should my papers (yellowed with their age)
Be scorned, like old men of less truth then tongue,
And your true rights be termed a Poet's rage,
And stretched metre of an Antique song.

This quatrain is fairly straightforward in meaning, with the additional meanings invested in words such as "tongue" and "rights" not contributing much to the overall sense. "Rage", however, was invested with more meaning than what it invokes today: "madness" and "insanity", for a start, but more importantly "spirit" and "passion" from the Old French - according to the lengthy note on **shakespeares-sonnets.com**, "Poet's frenzy" was a well-known state and was equated to the divine inspiration of a seer.

From the scans of the original publication that I'm working off, from **https://archive.org/details/shakespearessonn00shakrich**, the sonnets appear to have either been printed on yellow pages, or they really have yellowed with age. In the first case, then, line 9 would be ironic; in the second, it would be prescient.

"Stretched meter of an antique song" is an intriguing line. "Stretched" meant "extended", or "lengthened by force", which is clear in this instance, but less obviously referred to "being laid out for burial", and "exaggerated beyond proper limits". The capitalised "Antique" seems straightforward in meaning, but as it turns out was pronounced differently from the French until the turn of the 18th century, and in Shakespeare's day would have been read as "antic", which added the meanings of "grotesque" and "bizarre", and when referring to art: "fantastical figures, incongruously combined". All of this presents a complex and powerful range of images that tie in to the established themes.

> *But were some child of yours alive that time,*
> *You should live twice in it, and in my rhyme.*

In addition to "agreement in terminal sounds", and "poetic rhythm", the word "Rime" in Middle English was still used to mean "to reason" and "to count" - as in the expression "rhyme or reason" - which was a leftover from the Old English where the word "Rim" meant "number".

The accepted modernised text has an additional comma separate "in it" from "twice", and as counting is important to the sequence it should be noted that with the original punctuation "you" can live twice in the child in question *in addition* to living in the rhyme.

If Shakespeare had a living child he would continue to live through them, but after the death of Hamnet the longest he could hope for this to be the case would be until his last child had died, with no further continuation of his name. Even without children, however, he will continue to live on in the sonnet sequence, in its reasoned arguments and reflections, in its auditing and accounting of the Bard's spirit and legacy, and in the breath the reader lends to the words on these yellowed pages.

SONNET 18

1609 QUARTO VERSION

SHall I compare thee to a Summers day?
Thou art more louely and more temperate:
Rough windes do ſhake the darling buds of Maie,
And Sommers leaſe hath all too ſhorte a date:
Sometime too hot the eye of heauen ſhines,
And often is his gold complexion dimm'd,
And euery faire from faire ſome-time declines,
By chance, or natures changing courſe vntrim'd:
But thy eternall Sommer ſhall not fade,
Nor looſe poſſeſſion of that faire thou ow'ſt,
Nor ſhall death brag thou wandr'ſt in his ſhade,
When in eternall lines to time thou grow'ſt,
So long as men can breathe or eyes can ſee,
So long liues this, and this giues life to thee,

ANALYSIS

Just like its predecessor, sonnet 18 is a communication primarily between the sonnet and its creator.

Whether it is the sonnet or Shakespeare himself being compared to a summer's day, the sonnets that capture Shakespeare's youth will retain their potency as long as readers have eyes to read them and breath to speak them, while Shakespeare will earn immunity from old age and death as long as they continue to capture our imaginations and they have captured his soul.

> *Shall I compare thee to a Summer's day?*
> *Thou art more lovely and more temperate:*
> *Rough winds do shake the darling buds of May,*
> *And Summer's lease hath all too short a date:*

The first word that needs to be examined here is "temperate": meanings of "self-restrained, not swayed by passion" and "not liable to excessive heat or cold" may be clear, but the origin of the word is "temper", which might reference Latin's "tempus", meaning "time or season", but of particular usefulness relates to regulation, in line with the legal theme, and "tuning the pitch of a musical instrument", which continues the musical theme.

Before the 18th century, "winds" would have been pronounced "woinds" (rhyming more with "kinds"), and as early as the 15th century would have been loaded with additional meanings. The first would be "breath", "in speaking" in particular, which ties in to the reader's breathing of the sonnets being responsible for sounding the music of the words and for the shaking of the buds. The second, "moving by turning and twisting", relates to "wandering", and in turn to line 11's "wander'st" and the "wandering bark" of sonnet 116.

To add to that, the words "wind", "winds" or "windy" only appear 5 times in the sequence, in sonnets 14, 18, 51, 90 and 117, and at least three of those times in context of travelling.

"And Summer's lease", while sensible here, is originally written "And Sommers lease". In Old French, "sommer" meant "to count" or "add up", tying in with the accounting theme and lending the word "lease" an interesting qualification.

> *Sometime too hot the eye of heaven shines,*
> *And often is his gold complexion dimmed,*
> *And every fair from fair some-time declines,*
> *By chance, or nature's changing course untrimmed:*

"The eye of heaven" is the sun, and recalls the "I in heaven" from sonnet 14: the opening lines of this quatrain provide the reader with examples demonstrating the inconsistency of the sun's warmth. I strongly suspect that "the eye of heaven" is a reference to the all-seeing eye, the eye of Horus, which is referenced both in Greek mythology in the hymns of Orpheus and in Christianity in the forms of "Eye of Providence" or "Eye of God".

"Complexion" originally meant "temperament" and "natural disposition of body or mind"; in Middle English, the meaning derived from then-contemporary medicine was "bodily constitution or general nature resulting from blending of the four primary qualities (hot, cold, dry, moist) or humors (blood, phlegm, choler, black choler)".

This returns us to the study of alchemy, which I initially considered when reviewing the distillation theme of sonnet 5 and the refiguring of sonnet 6. According to the Islamic alchemist Jabir, lead was cold and dry while gold was hot and moist, so an alchemical sense of "gold complexion" would fit the context of sonnet 18 quite nicely.

"Fair", as discussed previously, can be read as "beauty", as "just", as "passage" and as "make" or "made".

"Declines", derived from Old French, meant "to sink", "decline", "degenerate", "turn aside", and "to deviate": two of those terms can refer to the sonnets sailing the ocean of eternity. The modern sense of "decline", "to refuse" or "not consent", only appears to have come into use a decade or two after the sonnets were published, so I doubt that that's relevant.

"Course" generally referred to an order, sequence, or "line in which something moves". From the late 14th century, "courses" was used for the flow of bodily fluids and "humors" which again relates to the gold complexion.

"Trim", by the late 16th century, was an evocative nautical term that meant "to be firm, solid, steadfast" and "to stabilise", to "distribute the load of a ship so she floats on an even keel", and was also the non-nautical term for "decorate" or "adorn".

To re-read the second quatrain with all of this in mind: the sun, the sun god, or Shakespeare, with time varies in his presence and in his qualities; eventually beauty ages, fair becomes unfair, what is made is unmade, the sun sets, and ships sink or sail off course, whether by luck or design, quite possibly by a change in the sonnet sequence or its undirected voyage into the unknown.

> *But thy eternal Summer shall not fade,*
> *Nor lose possession of that fair thou ow'st,*
> *Nor shall death brag thou wander'st in his shade,*
> *When in eternal lines to time thou grow'st,*

"Ow'st" is usually explained as both "owe" and "own", but it's the first meaning that I'm inclined to buy into as it follows the theme of usury, or money lending.

"That fair thou ow'st" can also be understood to be "the cost of passage that you owe".

I find it intriguing that in the Arden Sonnets, Katherine Duncan-Jones states that "The word growest may seem inapplicable to poetry", where it is my understanding that Shakespeare's sonnets do grow in time: both while Shakespeare is writing them, and in the sense that their spirit matures to self-awareness as the sequence progresses. It is possible, too, that the intention of "growing" was for the sonnets to increase in popularity and to continue to be published.

The beauty that Shakespeare has invested in the sonnets will remain in his possession in the form of the sonnets, just as the beauty that the sonnets impart to the reader will remain theirs. In this regard, the sonnets owe their beauty both to Shakespeare and to the reader, whereas Shakespeare owes it to himself and his son's memory to share it with the world.

Lines 11 and 12 evoke a wonderful image of Father Time, in spite of his propensity to relegate the dead to history, marching on accompanied by the ever-living poet embedded in the sonnet sequence.

> *So long as men can breathe or eyes can see,*
> *So long lives this, and this gives life to thee,*

The general meaning of the closing couplet of this famous sonnet is well-understood, but now that we have a much more nuanced understanding of the sonnet's intent we can see, four centuries later, that Shakespeare's sonnets have succeeded in their mission. We may not be reading them correctly, and we may even be sullying the reputation of the greatest figure in the history of literature, but the words of the sonnets continue to penetrate our hearts and escape our lips.

The Bard lives on, hiding in the ink trenches of the pages of the sonnets, imprinted on the hearts and in the minds of their readers.

SONNET 19

1609 QUARTO VERSION

DEuouring time blunt thou the Lyons pawes,
And make the earth deuoure her owne ſweet brood,
Plucke the keene teeth from the fierce Tygers yawes,
And burne the long liu'd Phœnix in her blood,
Make glad and ſorry ſeaſons as thou fleet'ſt,
And do what ere thou wilt ſwift-footed time
To the wide world and all her fading ſweets:
But I forbid thee one moſt hainous crime,
O carue not with thy howers my loues faire brow,
Nor draw noe lines there with thine antique pen,
Him in thy courſe vntainted doe allow,
For beauties patterne to ſucceding men.
Yet doe thy worſt ould Time diſpight thy wrong,
My loue ſhall in my verſe euer liue young.

ANALYSIS

Sonnet 19 is a plea from Shakespeare and his sonnet reflection to Father Time, who is both Chronos and the Grim Reaper.

> *Devouring Time, blunt thou the lion's paws,*
> *And make the earth devour her own sweet brood;*
> *Pluck the keen teeth from the fierce tiger's jaws,*
> *And burn the long-lived phoenix in her blood;*

In the modernised text, "time" has been capitalised and "devouring" highlighted as an adjective or epithet; "time" was not capitalised in the 1609 quarto text, however, nor was there a comma, and so we can read this both as addressing Father Time who oversees the ageing and passing of even the most powerful and long-lived creations, but also as a suggestion that Shakespeare's sonnets are devouring time, protecting his spirit from the beasts, the earthly grave, and outliving even the phoenix.

The lion is likely a reference to the constellation Leo, mentioned by Phoebus as one of the obstacles that his son Phaethon would have to contend with, or it may possibly be a biblical reference to the first Peter, chapter 5, which speaks of the devil as a roaring lion, "seeking whom he may devour".

Over time, whatever the earth produces will return to the soil, and while this might be an oblique reference to Chronos devouring his children I believe it's simply a continuation of the theme of tombs and graves.

Although we're familiar with the story of the phoenix being reborn in fire, in book 15 of Ovid's Metamorphoses it is described as dying and being reborn in a nest full of spices. I'm not certain whether this is of any relevance, but regardless of what Arthur Golding translated the fire version that we're familiar with today was well-known back then.

I find it interesting that the lion, the tiger and the phoenix are each only mentioned once in the sequence, here, especially seeing as the phoenix is such an important symbol referenced from Shakespeare's poem "The Phoenix and the Turtle".

> *Make glad and sorry seasons as thou fleet'st,*
> *And do whate'er thou wilt, swift-footed Time,*
> *To the wide world and all her fading sweets;*
> *But I forbid thee one most heinous crime:*

While the meaning of this quatrain is straightforward, there are a few words I'd like to mention that add some flavour.

"Fleet" as an adjective meant "swift", but as a verb meant to "fade" or "vanish", and would probably have been recognised in Shakespeare's day as a reference to ships. More interestingly, Fleet Street in London was known for printing and publishing and so this simple word "fleet'st" may be conflating all of these notions which connect to the established themes of time speeding by, ink and printing, and sailing and vanishing over the horizon.

Where the modernised text says "whate'er", the original text is "what ere". Of course this can be read as "whatever" to say that Time can do whatever it wishes, but the original text also allows for a reading of the word "ere" as "before". In this case, the reader can get the sense of "do what you want, Time, before you fade and vanish". Although we still have the sense of "whatever", this reading suggests the idea that time is finite, leading inexorably on towards Judgement Day.

"Sweets" would have meant both "pleasing things" and "beloved ones".

> *O! carve not with thy hours my love's fair brow,*
> *Nor draw no lines there with thine antique pen;*
> *Him in thy course untainted do allow*
> *For beauty's pattern to succeeding men.*

This quatrain is interesting as it positions Time as the writer and our world as the poetry, almost like the story of The Matrix for the turn of the 17th century: that is the precise nature of reality from the perspective of Shakespeare's spirit in the sonnets. This quatrain is ambiguous, and serves as a plea to time both to release Shakespeare's love, his spirit buried in the sonnets, from the effects of time, but also as a plea to preserve Shakespeare himself; in both cases, by allowing the text to survive unmolested.

It is sadly ironic, then, that with John Benson's 1640 republication of the sonnets that is precisely the hateful crime that Time committed; for almost four hundred years Shakespeare's reputation and legacy have been tainted, the meaning behind his sonnets perverted into little more than a sexually suggestive but highly artful series of missives to fictitious lovers. I find it tragically fascinating that through his sonnets, Shakespeare's words seem to anticipate so much of how his verse has been treated.

> *Yet, do thy worst old Time: despite thy wrong,*
> *My love shall in my verse ever live young.*

Here the sonnet turns from concern to confidence, and, as history would have it, rightly so. The value in Shakespeare's sonnets is not in how we read them, but that we read them at all, and Shakespeare had faith that we would not only continue to read his poetry, but that some day we would look back through the centuries and see him again, young and full of love, sorrow, beauty and wisdom, and that we would agree to open our mouths and lend him our voices.

SONNET 20

1609 QUARTO VERSION

A Womans face with natures owne hande painted,
Haſte thou, the Maſter Miſtris of my paſſion,
A womans gentle hart but not acquainted
With ſhifting change as is falſe womens faſhion,
An eye more bright then theirs, leſſe falſe in rowling:
Gilding the obiect where-vpon it gazeth,
A man in hew all Hews in his controwling,
Which ſteales mens eyes and womens ſoules amaſeth,
And for a woman wert thou firſt created,
Till nature as ſhe wrought thee fell a dotinge,
And by addition me of thee defeated,
By adding one thing to my purpoſe nothing.
But ſince ſhe prickt thee out for womens pleaſure,
Mine be thy loue and thy loues vſe their treaſure.

ANALYSIS

I will introduce sonnet 20 with a quote from Arthur Golding's translation of Ovid's Metamorphoses. you can find this quote on page 73 of Shakespeare's Ovid, which is available in the Appendix. The following lines describe Narcissus' first contact with his own reflection:

> *His ardent eyes which like two starres full bright and shyning bee,*
> *And eke his fingars, fingars such as Bacchus might beseeme,*
> *And haire that one might worthely Apollos haire it deeme.*
> *His beardlesse chinne and yvorie necke, and eke the perfect grace*
> *Of white and red indifFerently bepainted in his face.*
> *All these he woondreth to beholde, for which (as I doe gather)*
> *Himselfe was to be wondred at, or to be pitied rather.*
> *He is enamored of himselfe for want of taking heede.*
> *And where he lykes another thing, he lykes himselfe in deede.*
> *He is the partie whome he wooes, and suter that doth wooe,*
> *He is the flame that settes on fire, and thing that burneth tooe.*

While exploring Ovid's Metamorphoses for references from sonnet 20's second quatrain, I discovered the original story of Pyramus and Thisbe, and, I'm ashamed to admit, it was for the very first time. Not only is the tragedy of Pyramus and Thisbe the basis for the story of Romeo and Juliet, and not only is it so callously ruined by the mechanicals in A Midsummer Night's Dream, but it might also be serving as an underlying theme for Shakespeare's sonnets, with Shakespeare in the role of Pyramus, the reader in the role of Thisbe, and the sonnets serving as the hole in the wall between them that allows the two to communicate their love. Additionally, the "master mistress" of sonnet 20's first quatrain might be a reference to the story of Hermaphroditus, in which a naiad falls in love with the godlike youth and forces him to merge with her in a sexless union.

Now that the stage has been set, we can begin:

> *A woman's face with nature's own hand painted,*
> *Hast thou, the Master Mistress of my passion,*
> *A woman's gentle heart but not acquainted*
> *With shifting change as is false women's fashion,*

This sonnet returns to the pattern of addressing all three members of the sonnet trinity: Shakespeare himself, his sonnet reflection, and the reader. Shakespeare is using black ink to paint both his sonnet reflection and a picture of the imagined reader, and the sonnets are addressing both Shakespeare and the reader. If we read the sonnet out loud to the sonnet, it presents some additional interesting possibilities.

The first line can be read both as "a woman's face painted as a man's" and "a man's face painted as a woman's". The sonnets are reflections of Shakespeare, who is the Narcissus of the sonnet narrative, but they are written primarily for the female reader, or Echo. The sonnet caught in the middle of this communication plays both man to their reader and woman to their creator.

Painting something black, at the time Shakespeare wrote the sonnets, implied to "represent it as wicked or evil". As the conceit of representation with black ink is a major theme running through the sonnets, I consider it highly probable that Shakespeare thought of his efforts to invest the sonnets with his soul as "black magic".

The word "master" has a rich and varied history, and the meanings that are relevant and which were available at the time the sonnets were written are as follows: "a man having control or authority", "owner of a living creature", "a dominant woman", a "young gentleman", or a boy of better class but too young to be called "mister".

Shakespeare is the master of his sonnets in the sense of his authority as creator and - relating to the established husbandry theme - owner of the sonnets as "living creatures". The female reader is a "dominant woman" in that she brings the sonnets to life or returns them to their eternal darkness whenever she opens or closes the book, and the sonnets are Shakespeare's little sons, too young for the title "mister" but certainly of high enough class for the title "master".

"Mistress" in the 16th century had a few mostly positive meanings, but in my opinion here primarily serves to clarify the irrelevance of assigning a gender to the addressee.

"Passion" recalls the word "rage" from sonnet 17, tempered by "temperate" in sonnet 18, and invokes both the passion of a poet writing passionately, and Shakespeare's grief and frustration over the loss of his son Hamnet.

In the phrase "a woman's gentle hart", "gentle" meant "mild", "tender" and "noble". We can read the word "heart" both metaphorically, and as a "stag", or "male red deer". This second meaning might be a reference either to Narcissus hunting or to the husbandry theme. Whether that's valid or not, we can safely stick to reading this as a metaphorical heart, meaning "the soul" or "emotional muscle".

"Shifting change" is a tautology, here reinforcing the idea that the sonnets are static, frozen in time, eternally constant and faithful.

"Fashion" did mean "prevailing custom", "mode of dress" and "adornment prevailing in a place and time", but also "physical make-up or composition", "form", "shape" and "appearance", and in Old French had the additional meanings of "face", "pattern", "design", "thing done", "beauty", "manner" and "characteristic feature". The sonnets are fashioned by Shakespeare's passion, imagination, ink and quill; "woman" in Old English referred to both sexes and living people's appearances and natures are subject to change as they grow older and wiser.

Assuming that Shakespeare intended a pun on the word "acquainted" to mean "having a vagina", "but not acquainted" then ties in to "prickt thee out" in the closing couplet of the sonnet.

That's a lot of detail for one quatrain, so let's take a moment to summarise these readings:

For Shakespeare, the sonnet, whether imagined as male or female, was written as a receptacle for his self-love and as a vehicle for carrying his love to the reader, with a tender, gentle heart that is constant and unshifting.

For the sonnet, Shakespeare is the master and the reader is the mistress, with both being addressed in the second person. Shakespeare has a gentle heart, he has a woman's spirit with a man's temperament, and in spending two decades infusing his legacy into the sonnet sequence he most certainly demonstrates that he is faithful, dedicated and unwavering.

The reader, on the other hand, is the ungendered "master mistress" whose decision to read or continue reading the sonnet sequence determines whether Shakespeare's spirit sees the light of day or remains trapped in the eternal darkness of the closed book. Regardless of whether the reader is subject to whims, as long as they are reading the sonnets they are due all praise, in this case paid out in the form of flattery.

> *An eye more bright than theirs, less false in rolling,*
> *Gilding the object where-upon it gazeth:*
> *A man in hue all Hues in his controlling,*
> *Which steals men's eyes and women's souls amazeth,*

The straightforward reading of the word "rolling" in context of an eye - understood both then and today as being done in exasperation, annoyance, disbelief or impatience - is accompanied by its evocation of the sound of rolling thunder, tying into the musical theme, and probably was a hint to the sonnet being written on a rolled up piece of parchment or paper. It is also a very rare word in Golding's translation of Ovid's Metamorphoses, and there are a few expressions in sonnet 20 that lead me to suspect that this quatrain is referencing the story of Atalanta from book 10, wherein Hippomenes wins their race and her love by tricking her with golden apples.

The word "hew", due in part to its suspicious spelling in the original quarto text, sent me on a surprisingly long and fruitful investigation. To "hew" in the original spelling meant to "cut evenly", and "stick to a course", the former recalling the lines of text being cut into the sonnet page and the latter recalling the sailing and navigation theme.

In its modernised spelling - and here we must recall that although the sonnets are written art, they are intended to be spoken aloud - "hue" meant "outcry", or "noise" from Old French, which became "outcry calling for pursuit of a felon", and by Shakespeare's day had evolved into "cry of alarm". Prior to the 17th century, when the word "colour" became the dominant meaning of the word "hue", it still evoked "colour", "form", "appearance", "species", "kind" and "beauty", and it is used in the Metamorphoses translation to describe Narcissus' cheeks that had been white and red before he was torn apart by grief.

Having said all that, from the sonnet point of view the second quatrain describes Shakespeare making his work more golden and valuable the longer he looked at it. Shakespeare became a man - in appearance to the reader - composed of all the appearances (or sonnets) under his control, and the sonnets would capture the hearts and imaginations of male and female readers alike. The reader, from the other side of the looking glass, is praised as having a bright and faithful eye, as investing the sonnet with value by reading it; in this case the "man in hew" would be the object being gazed at, and so the meaning of the last two lines would not change.

> *And for a woman wert thou first created,*
> *Till nature as she wrought thee fell a-doting,*
> *And by addition me of thee defeated,*
> *By adding one thing to my purpose nothing.*

"Addition" meant "increase" and "augmentation" in Old French.

"Defeated" meant to "bring ruination", or "cause destruction", and to "frustrate", or "prevent the success of".

We can read this quatrain as saying that Shakespeare initially created this sonnet for women's eyes, but then fell in love with it himself; by adding self-love to "me of thee", this sonnet of Shakespeare, the sequence's original purpose has been compromised.

We can also read it from the sonnet's perspective addressing Shakespeare, suggesting that Shakespeare was originally created for a woman, until nature interfered with that purpose, possibly by bringing about the the death of Hamnet. If that's a valid hypothesis, then each sonnet would be an addition that steers Shakespeare further off-course from his original "naturally intended" purpose.

> *But since she prick'd thee out for women's pleasure,*
> *Mine be thy love and thy love's use their treasure.*

Sonnet 20 is a play on Narcissus declaring his love for his reflection, which visually reflects and responds to his love even though it cannot act or speak independently. The same could be said for Hermaphroditus, to whom the naiad attached herself in spite of the fact that he was innocently going about his business and trying to enjoy a swim. In similar fashion, the sonnet reflects Shakespeare's love, useless to him sexually, and yet wholly true and full of passion.

I'd like to take a moment to play a game of "What if?". What if this sonnet was addressed to Hamnet? What if Shakespeare was exaggerating Hamnet's qualities to align them with an idealised, kinder version of Narcissus? Hamnet was certainly the "master mistress" of Shakespeare's desperate passion to preserve his legacy in the sonnet sequence. What if the "thee" of "me of thee" refers to Hamnet, with Shakespeare's legacy frustrated by his addition to Shakespeare's lineage and then tragic death?

Regardless, the sonnets are geared, or "prickt out", to give pleasure to women, whom Shakespeare presumes will be the readers of the sonnets; the poem attached to the sonnet sequence, "A Lover's Complaint", informs us of Shakespeare's predicted outcome for his sonnets: as long as women read these sonnets as the intended addressees, the love carried by the sonnet will be revived both for Shakespeare and the sonnets, and their love's use, the reading of the sonnets, will become the reader's treasure.

SONNET 21

1609 QUARTO VERSION

SO is it not with me as with that Muſe,
Stird by a painted beauty to his verſe,
Who heauen it ſelfe for ornament doth vſe,
And euery faire with his faire doth reherſe,
Making a coopelment of proud compare
With Sunne and Moone,with earth and ſeas rich gems:
With Aprills first borne flowers and all things rare,
That heauens ayre in this huge rondure hems,
O let me true in loue but truly write,
And then beleeue me,my loue is as faire,
As any mothers childe,though not ſo bright
As thoſe gould candells fixt in heauens ayre:
Let them ſay more that like of heare-ſay well,
I will not prayſe that purpoſe not to ſell.

ANALYSIS

In the Arden Sonnets it's proposed that this sonnet is inspired by Philip Sidney's Astrophil and Stella, which is entirely likely, and a lot of the commentary surrounds Shakespeare's deliberate use of exaggerated poetic style as a means of making fun of the efforts of other poets.

While that certainly sets a snarky tone for sonnet 21, the narrative doesn't suffer for it; my usual word-search through Golding's translation of Ovid's Metamorphoses turned up a few interesting plots from book 10, and the stories of Cyparisssus and Hyacinthus are certainly referenced by a number of Shakespeare's sonnets, whether or not this one does directly.

> *So is it not with me as with that Muse,*
> *Stirred by a painted beauty to his verse,*
> *Who heaven it self for ornament doth use,*
> *And every fair with his fair doth rehearse,*

Shakespeare is the Muse of the sonnets and his muse would be the conflation of his lost son and this sonnet. Both Shakespeare and the sonnets are painted beauties, Shakespeare being painted, or written, into the sonnet and the sonnet being painted by Shakespeare.

Once again, "fair" can mean a number of things, but usually seems to imply "to make" or "made" from the French "faire" and here makes sense as a reference to the creature / creation theme.

"Rehearse" had a few meanings in Shakespeare's day: from the Old French it meant "to give an account of", which ties in with a number of established themes, and from the mid-14th century meant "to say over again", or "repeat what has already been said or written". This is what the sonnets will do for all eternity, or at least as long as there are readers who read them out loud. What's of particular interest to me, however, is that in Old French the word "rehearse" also meant "to rake over", or "turn over", the former returning us to the husbandry theme and the latter possibly referring to the turning of the pages as we read.

So here in the first quatrain we have Shakespeare declaring that he's not like the poet that's inspired him, while ironically contradicting himself. It is possible, however, that "so is it not with me" might be read instead as literal, not as "so is it not the case with me" but rather "it does not reside with me", where "it" might be referring to Shakespeare's or Hamnet's spirit.

> *Making a couplement of proud compare*
> *With Sun and Moon, with earth and sea's rich gems:*
> *With April's first-born flowers and all things rare,*
> *That heaven's air in this huge rondure hems,*

"Proud" in Old French meant "brave, valiant" and in Old English "excellent", "splendid", "arrogant", or "haughty", but, intriguingly, in Latin "prode" meant "advantageous" or "profitable" and this resonates with the closing couplet of this sonnet.

"Compare" might still have been understood as "regard or treat as equal" in addition to its modern-day meaning.

"Gem", from "sea's rich gems", meant "a precious stone" as it does today, and also "a rare or excellent example". It may also have been a reference to its Latin root, meaning "eye".

If the sonnets are travelling the sea of eternity, they will be in the company of many other great works of art that have survived the ravages of time. The sonnet sequence would be comparable to these other works, and they are most certainly a rare and excellent example of Shakespeare's skill and spirit. The sonnets, as I've mentioned many times before, also serve as Shakespeare's "eyes" in context of the overarching narrative of Narcissus and Echo, as reflections of his ego and identity, and as windows into his soul.

In the Arden Sonnets, it's suggested that the "air" of "heaven's air" may be a pun on "heir", which would be Shakespeare's lost heir, Hamnet, and his replacement, the sonnet sequence.

"Rondure" was a fancy way of saying "roundness", and heaven's air "hems", which meant "to enclose" or "circumscribe".

The first quatrain's rehearsal produces a wonderful "couplement" in the second quatrain that is comparable to the heavenly bodies, the physical world, our greatest works, the first spring bloom in all its potential, and everything rare that our planet's atmosphere - and Shakespeare's sonnet sequence - contains.

> *O! let me true in love but truly write,*
> *And then believe me, my love is as fair,*
> *As any mother's child, though not so bright*
> *As those gold candles fixed in heaven's air:*

Sonnet 130, the famous sonnet beginning "My mistress' eyes are nothing like the sun", is referred to in at least two ways by sonnet 21: "And then believe me, my love is as fair" anticipates sonnet 130's "And yet by heaven, I think my love as rare", just as the closing couplet's "Let them say more that like of hearsay well" ties in to "As any she belied with false compare".

I noticed that connection before reading through the commentary in the Arden Sonnets; for Katherine Duncan-Jones, what connects the two sonnets is the phrase "those gold candles" which is mentioned as "a possible allusion to Sidney's identification of the subject of his sonnet sequence as 'Stella', or Star."

I believe that there are two ways to read the third quatrain: the traditional way, in which "my love is as fair / as any mothers child" is meaningless because what's being contrasted is a human being to any other human being, or alternatively with the idea that the sonnet is the object of Shakespeare's affection, in which case these lines become profoundly changed and Shakespeare is declaring that his love for his embedded reflections is as strong as for any real child, even if they're painted black, even if they're not as bright as Sydney's Stella, even if they're not as bright as the "eye more bright" from sonnet 20,

Hamnet, who is the golden sun (and son) of Shakespeare and the sonnet sequence.

> *Let them say more that like of hear-say well,*
> *I will not praise that purpose not to sell.*

"Sell" was a surprisingly versatile word in the 16th century: while in Shakespeare's day it became the slang for "to swindle", it still meant "to give", "lend", "supply" and "deliver" from Old English and the expression "to sell one's soul" was a relatively new invention.

I mentioned before that the "hearsay" may be a reference to sonnet 130's "false compare", but I believe there's a lot more to this, particularly because in the original text the word is hyphenated as "heare-say" which allows for other interpretations.

The "them" that say more could refer to the sonnets, who appreciate the reader's reading aloud, or the readers, who enjoy the game of reading the sonnets aloud and hearing Shakespeare's words coming out of their own mouths.

This closing couplet is traditionally read as "I will not flatter what I don't intend to sell", but with the older meanings of "sell" and a positive interpretation of the term "heare-say", I think we can understand it in a different way: "I encourage the readers to keep reading and the sonnets to keep being read, but I will not give praise to anyone, sonnet or human, that does not intend to pass on my legacy".

SONNET 22

1609 QUARTO VERSION

MY glaſſe ſhall not perſwade me I am ould,
So long as youth and thou are of one date,
But when in thee times forrwes I behould,
Then look I death my daies ſhould expiate.
For all that beauty that doth couer thee,
Is but the ſeemely rayment of my heart,
Which in thy breſt doth liue,as thine in me,
How can I then be elder than thou art?
O therefore loue be of thy ſelfe ſo wary,
As I not for my ſelfe,but for thee will,
Bearing thy heart which I will keepe ſo chary
As tender nurſe her babe from faring ill,
Preſume not on thy heart when mine is ſlaine,
Thou gau'ſt me thine not to giue backe againe.

ANALYSIS

shakespeares-sonnets.com has a lengthy comment for sonnet 22 discussing the significance of the sonnets that are numbered as multiples of 11, and while I'm sure that's correct I haven't yet seen how the number 22 fits in. What I am certain of is that this sonnet is fully readable as being addressed to Shakespeare, to the sonnet, and to the reader.

> *My glass shall not persuade me I am old,*
> *So long as youth and thou are of one date,*
> *But when in thee time's furrows I behold,*
> *Then look I death my days should expiate.*

Throughout the sequence, "my glass" is the looking glass that reflects, and Shakespeare and his sonnets both see the other as being on the reflected side of it. Through the glass of the sonnets, the reader can see Shakespeare's reflection while the sonnets see the reader both on his behalf and through the reader's own eyes.

"Persuade" means "bring over by talking". "Youth" may or may not be a pun meaning "you-ness".

"Date" seems like it might be interesting, but it's not clear if the Old French meaning still recalled its Latin origin "to give", "grant" or "offer".

"Furrows" was written "forrwes" in the original text, and while I'm a hard sell that "furrows" was the only way it was meant to be read, I so far haven't found any fitting alternatives myself.

"Expiate" means "atone for", or "make amends", but originally meant to "extinguish" or "put an end to".

In the Arden Sonnets, "then look I death" is translated to "then I anticipate death", but I believe the word "look" here is important: whoever is speaking is not simply anticipating death, but looking at death's reflection; they are both seeing an image, and seeing themselves reflected as they "look", or "appear". Even today, "look to" means "see to" or "be sure to", and combined with the word "should" this becomes a conditional instruction to Shakespeare or the sonnet: "if I see you in time's furrows, then I should ensure that death expiates my days" or "that my days expiate my death". I had to read that line quite a few times before I realised that the order of the words "death" and "my daies" is actually ambiguous.

For Shakespeare, this opening quatrain is saying that he will not be discouraged by his physical mirror as long as his youth is still reflected in the sonnet, but when he sees the passage of time in the lines of the sonnet's text and his old age before him then he is compelled to ensure that his death and legacy will make amends for his life.

For the sonnet speaking to Shakespeare, Shakespeare's age will not affect him as long as Shakespeare and the youth captured in the sonnet were born on the same day; but when the sonnet witnesses Shakespeare ageing it is compelled to ensure that its days will atone for the Bard's death.

When the reader is addressed, then the youth and the reader will no longer be "of one date": at this point the sonnet's "days", the times when the book is open and the reader is reading it, must be used to atone for Shakespeare's death as effectively as possible.

> *For all that beauty that doth cover thee,*
> *Is but the seemly raiment of my heart,*
> *Which in thy breast doth live, as thine in me,*
> *How can I then be elder than thou art?*

While "raiment" was a word for dress, it was derived from the Old French "array", which meant "order", "position", "arrangement", or "sequence" as well as "rank or line of soldiers". The sonnet sequence is an array that clothes Shakespeare's embedded spirit, and there's also a reference to the lines of verse in military terms that recalls the trenches from sonnet 2 and the sap from sonnet 5. It's also possible that there's a pun intended on the word "ray", as in rays of the sun.

The phrasing of the two lines "the seemly raiment of my heart / which in thy brest doth live" is ambiguous: we can read it as stating that the beauty, or raiment, is what lives in "thy breast", or that the heart covered by the raiment is what lives there. Either meaning works well.

"Art", as before, can be read both in its modernised sense of "are", a state of being, and as "art", where the sonnet being addressed is art that Shakespeare has produced or where "art" is the verb for the act of Shakespeare producing it.

When addressed from Shakespeare to the sonnet, the second quatrain is saying that for all the beautiful words that Shakespeare has invested in the sonnet, they are only words forming the outer appearance of his spirit; as Shakespeare's spirit itself lives on in the sonnet's breast, as it does in him, how can Shakespeare be any older than the sonnet, or the youth captured in it?

When addressed to Shakespeare, the sonnet is saying that with all the beauty that Shakespeare has (and remember, Shakespeare in the sonnet context is Narcissus), it's only the surface of what the sonnet and Shakespeare truly share: his spirit. The sonnet questions how it could be older than Shakespeare, and while it's strange to think about, if we look at the sonnet as a snapshot in time and Shakespeare as being in the present during his reading of the sonnet, then even mere moments after Shakespeare had written the sonnet it would already have been older than him, in the sense that it would be of a previous time.

When addressed to the reader, we can imagine the sonnet covering the reader with its beauty while it is being read, and that it is the beauty and Shakespeare's spirit that live in the sonnet's and the reader's hearts. even though the sonnet, especially nowadays, is considerably older than the reader, they will be of one date for the duration of the reading experience.

> *O! therefore love be of thy self so wary,*
> *As I not for my self, but for thee will,*
> *Bearing thy heart which I will keep so chary*
> *As tender nurse her babe from faring ill,*

"Will", as usual in the sonnet sequence, is ambiguous, both meaning "I will for thee be wary" and also "as I will be for thee, William".

"Chary" meant "sorrowful", "full of care" and "careful".

The words "bearing" and "faring ill" recall the established sailing theme.

"Heart" in this context is a metaphor for soul, love, and spirit.

Shakespeare is cognisant of the fact that we tend to be a lot more compassionate towards others than we are towards ourselves, even more so towards people that we care about.

In the third quatrain, Shakespeare tells the sonnet, his love, to take care of itself in the way that Shakespeare cares not for himself, but for the sonnet. The sonnet bears its heart which Shakespeare will keep from misfortune, presumably through his art.

The sonnet, meanwhile, is wary not for its own sake, but for Shakespeare's. The sonnet bears Shakespeare's heart and keeps it carefully.

The reader is instructed to be wary: the sonnet does not care for itself, but for the reader and Will, its creator. It's even possible to read from this that the sonnet also "Will"s, or "becomes William", for the reader. When the sonnet tells the reader that it is bearing the reader's heart, it is positioning the reader as a passenger, and the reader's heart is borne by the sonnet on this journey through the sequence.

> *Presume not on thy heart when mine is slain,*
> *Thou gav'st me thine not to give back again.*

"Presume" meant "to take upon oneself", "to take liberty", "to take for granted" and to "presuppose".

"Slain" meant to "smite", "strike", or "beat". If the last meaning was intended then this might be a reference to a beating heart, or beating a drum in the sense of the established musical theme.

Shakespeare gave his heart to the sonnet to carry, and if the sonnet ever ceases to be read Shakespeare will not get it back again. The sonnet must not take its heart for granted once Shakespeare's stops beating; the sonnets are duty-bound, contracted to Shakespeare, and cannot go back on their obligation to their creator.

For the reader, "presume not on thy heart when mine is slain" may be read as "don't take your heart for granted, let my heart's failure be a lesson to you". Once the reader has given the sonnets their heart, or let the sonnets into their heart, there will be no going back: Shakespeare's heart beat until his death, the sonnet's heart repeats Shakespeare's beats whenever it is read, and the reader's soul once inspired by the sonnets will forever remain imprinted with the spirit of the bard.

SONNET 23

1609 QUARTO VERSION

AS an vnperfect actor on the ſtage,
Who with his feare is put beſides his part,
Or ſome fierce thing repleat with too much rage,
Whoſe ſtrengths abondance weakens his owne heart;
So I for feare of truſt, forget to ſay,
The perfect ceremony of loues right,
And in mine owne loues ſtrength ſeeme to decay,
Ore-charg'd with burthen of mine owne loues might:
O let my books be then the eloquence,
And domb preſagers of my ſpeaking breſt,
Who pleade for loue, and look for recompence,
More then that tonge that more hath more expreſt.
O learne to read what ſilent loue hath writ,
To heare wit eies belongs to loues fine wiht.

ANALYSIS

Sonnet 23 is precisely the kind of sonnet that frustrates me when I read others' analyses of it, in particular because contemporary interpretations rely on modifications to the original 1609 quarto text. After clearly establishing a theme of writing and reading in the 22 sonnets prior, some scholars have modernised the word "books" to "looks", which radically alters the meaning of that line and those that follow.

As I've said before, I don't believe that there is a single misprint in the entire sonnet sequence. I strongly believe that Shakespeare worked side-by-side with Thomas Thorpe to ensure the perfectly accurate printing of the only work of his that he would ever publish.

With that out of the way, sonnet 23 is another plea from Shakespeare and the sonnet to the reader requesting that the reader lend the sonnets their voice and read the sonnets out loud. The primary intention of this sonnet is relatively straightforward; for example, the first quatrain is discussing an untrained actor being thrust on stage into a role he hasn't prepared for. As in all the sonnets, however, there are additional layers that are well worth exploring.

> *As an unperfect actor on the stage,*
> *Who with his fear is put besides his part,*
> *Or some fierce thing replete with too much rage,*
> *Whose strength's abundance weakens his own heart;*

"Unperfect actor" implies not just a lack of mastery of the role, but not really being suited for the role in the first place.

The word "actor" meant "an overseer", "guardian", "steward", "an agent", someone engaged to "act on stage", "play the part of", or "plead a cause at law"; the sonnets are actors playing the role of Shakespeare, they are the guardians and stewards of Shakespeare's legacy, his spirit captured in text, and they serve as his agents and his legal representation in the court of public opinion.

The reader, however, is precisely "an unperfect actor" because they are thrust unprepared into the role of reading Shakespeare's lines out loud. They are also, as is qualified by sonnet 130's "My Mistress' eyes are nothing like the Sun", far from the ideals of beauty as dictated by traditional sonnet sequences.

A "stage" is a "raised platform used for public display", and also "the platform beneath the gallows", from the Old French; the sonnet sequence is a platform for public display of the sonnets, the stage on where they act, and it's where Shakespeare hangs them. Both of these meanings connect with established themes.

"Stage" also implied a "stage" or "rest" in a journey, and "period of development or time in life", and these are also relevant as the sonnets are travelling on a journey through eternity and each reader is a stop, a period of time that they can experience while briefly exposed to the light.

According to the Arden Sonnets "put beside his part" meant "forgets his lines" or "loses his mastery of his role": "part" was the technical term for the lines and cues to be learned by an actor.

Personally, I think it goes further and infers a separation between actor and role, with the actor being the sonnet and Shakespeare being the role, and the sonnets positioned literally beside the bard.

"Fierce" is a puzzling word as it originally meant "proud", "noble", "bold", or "haughty" from Old French but transformed into "ferocious", "wild", "savage", "cruel" and occasionally, in Shakespeare's day, was used as "dangerous", "destructive", "great", "strong" or "huge in number". It's important to note here that what's being described by the adjective "fierce" is "thing", and while contemporary interpretations of this consider it to mean a savage beast or human being, I'm of the opinion that the "fierce thing" full of the poet's passion is the text, this sonnet or the book of sonnets, recalling Hamlet's famous quote: "the play's the thing / Wherein I'll catch the conscience of the King". All the possible meanings of the word "fierce" are appropriate here, including that of "numerous".

The text is invested with the poet's "rage", which as previous sonnets have discussed needs to be tempered in order for their message to be communicated effectively. The abundance of strength weakening the poet's heart, or at least weakening the arguments of his heart, follows these reflections accordingly.

"Heart" here has been interpreted as "courage" and "determination", but, as has already been established (and which came up a few times in the previous sonnet) is also a metaphor for "the soul", "love", and "spirit". The more passion Shakespeare invests into his heart's reflection, the sonnets, the weaker his own heart becomes; this idea was introduced all the way back in the first sonnet with "Feed'st thy light's flame with self-substantial fuel / Making a famine where abundance lies". He even uses the same word, "abundance", to link these lines directly, a word that only appears four times throughout the entire sonnet sequence.

> *So I for fear of trust, forget to say,*
> *The perfect ceremony of love's rite,*
> *And in mine own love's strength seem to decay,*
> *Ore-charged with burthen of mine own love's might:*

"Fear" meant the same as it does today, but also carried the meaning of "feeling of dread and reverence for God", and I believe it's strongly connected to the earlier word "fierce" and the French "fier".

"Trust" is a loaded word, carrying "reliability", "trustworthiness", "fidelity", "faithfulness", "confident expectation", "that on which one relies", a legal sense of "confidence placed in a one who holds or enjoys the use of property entrusted to him by its legal owner" and the "condition of being legally entrusted". Those last two tie in to the established legal theme, but also work as a description of the sonnets as the legal entities holding and enjoying the words and ideas that their rightful owner has entrusted to them.

"Ceremony" meant "a religious observance" and "a solemn rite", but also "a mere formality" by the mid-16th century.

"Right" meant "just", "good", "fair", "proper", "fitting", "straight", "not bent", "direct", "erect", "honest", "true", and "correct". It was probably also a play on the word "rite", meaning "religious observance or ceremony", "custom", or "usage", which would render the line "The perfect ceremony of loues right" a tautology.

Katherine Duncan-Jones reads the modernised" o'ercharged with" as "weighed down with; and crushed with the 'charge' or responsibility", but I believe that the original text's spelling as "ore-charged" may have been intended to mean "charged with ink", the ingredients of which included iron sulphate and that's a detail with which I'm confident that Shakespeare would have been familiar. Iron sulphate played an important role in alchemy, and Shakespeare's sonnets are a form of alchemy; this is a theme that has been established since the "refiguring" discussed in sonnet 6. After running a search through the original text, this reading appears to be borne out in 13 other sonnets as well as "A Lover's Complaint": 5, 12, 30, 34, 65, 81, 82, 107, 108, 112, 118, 128 and 139. If I'm correct in this interpretation, then we can make a case for the ceremony, or rite, being a form of alchemy or spell-casting.

"Burthen" is an alternate way of saying "burden": originally it was "a load", "weight", "charge" or "duty"; but also "a child", and in Shakespeare's day included the sense of "refrain" or "chorus of a song", which originated in the 14th century's "bass accompaniment to music", from the Old French "bordon". In addition to the contemporary interpretation of this line as continuing the earlier comparison to an enraged beast, the implications of "a child" and "bass accompaniment" bring us back to the framing theme of the sonnets being "little sons", or replacements for Hamnet, and the musical theme established in sonnet 8 based on sonnets being "little songs".

From Shakespeare to the sonnet, the second quatrain would then read: "I, an actor, out of pride for what I have entrusted to you, and fear for it, forget to adhere to the formalities and traditions of love; the more of my strength I invest in you the closer I come to death, you are charged with ink and are the duteous song-child that is a product of the power of my love".

From the sonnet to the reader, the second quatrain reads: "I, an agent of Shakespeare, for fear of trusting you, forget to adhere to the formalities and traditions of love; I am so full of love that I seem to be in danger of self-destruction (coming across too strong to be believed), and I am ink-charged with the duty of carrying Shakespeare's power.

> *O! let my books be then the eloquence,*
> *And dumb presagers of my speaking breast,*
> *Who plead for love, and look for recompense,*
> *More then that tongue that more hath more express'd.*

"Book" meant "a main subdivision of a larger work", "writing", and "written document". Shakespeare's books - those he draws inspiration from, those he writes to, and especially his sonnets - will speak on his behalf. They are dumb, because written words cannot speak themselves, and they are portentous, ominous, informing the future and preceding and anticipating the audible speech of those that will read them.

In the Arden Sonnets, Katherine Duncan-Jones states that "'presage' normally carries connotations of foretelling the future, but in Venus and Adonis Shakespeare applied it to Adonis' silent blush, an 'ill presage' of the words he is about to speak".

Shakespeare himself would have read the words aloud after writing them, even if only to make sure that they sounded as intended. When we, the readers, read these words aloud, we read the words "dumb presagers of my speaking breast" from our own speaking breasts.

The words here in this sonnet are pleading for love and looking for reciprocation from the reader, which would serve as compensation for Shakespeare's efforts as established in the borrowing and lending theme from sonnet 4.

The word "tongue" means "tongue", "organ of speech", "speech", and "a people's language", and here applies to both the sonnet which serves as Shakespeare's tongue and the reader's literal tongue. The repetition of the word "more" in "More then that tongue that more hath more express'd" recalls the repetition of the phrase "ten times" from sonnet 6, and the last line of the third quatrain can be understood to be saying that the more words, the more sonnets, the more love and pleading for love would be expressed; the more experienced the reader's tongue, in general, or specifically in reciting the sonnets, the more love will be expressed and the more the act of reading will compensate Shakespeare for his investment.

> *O! learn to read what silent love hath writ,*
> *To hear with eyes belongs to love's fine wit.*

"Fine" meant "perfected" or "of highest quality" from Old French, which evolved to "rich", "valuable", "costly", "true", "genuine", "faithful", "constant", "expertly fashioned", "well or skilfully made" and "delicately wrought". All of these meanings fit well with established themes in describing Shakespeare's sonnets.

The Arden Sonnets suggests that "silent love" is a reference to Sidney's Astrophil and Stella's "Dumb swans, not chattering pies, do lovers prove; / They love indeed, who quake to say they love". It also states that "'to hear with eyes' negates the commonplace assertion that love is blind, instead, love is claimed to read or to discern with sharpened insight".

That's all well and good, but these lines contain something

much more profound, while literally much more superficial. The original 1609 quarto text presents a challenge to the reader, "to heare wit eies" and "belongs to loves fine wiht".

"Wit" meant "mental capacity" and "ability to connect ideas and express them in an amusing way". "Wiht", in the 16th century, was an alternate spelling to "whit" and meant "amount", usually a tiny amount, or "human being", and originated in the Old English word "wight" for "living being", "creature", "person", "something", "anything". As I repeated earlier, I do not for one second believe that Shakespeare's sonnets contain even a single misprint, and it is my opinion that the last line of this sonnet is intended to be a puzzle for the reader; the instruction is to "learn what silent love hath writ", and what silent love has written is the final line of this sonnet that must be read and spoken correctly in order to complete the perfect ceremony of love's rite that will seal the love between Shakespeare and the reader.

SONNET 24

1609 QUARTO VERSION

MIne eye hath play'd the painter and hath ſteeld,
Thy beauties forme in table of my heart,
My body is the frame wherein ti's held,
And perſpectiue it is beſt Painters art.
For through the Painter muſt you ſee his skill,
To finde where your true Image pictur'd lies,
Which in my boſomes ſhop is hanging ſtil,
That hath his windowes glazed with thine eyes:
Now ſee what good-turnes eyes for eies haue done,
Mine eyes haue drawne thy ſhape,and thine for me
Are windowes to my breſt, where-through the Sun
Delights to peepe,to gaze therein on thee
Yet eyes this cunning want to grace their art
They draw but what they ſee,know not the hart.

ANALYSIS

Before we begin to discuss the sonnet itself, I feel obligated to draw attention to the number 24, which I feel certain should be important considering that there are 24 hours in a day.

> *Mine eye hath played the painter and hath steeled,*
> *Thy beauty's form in table of my heart,*
> *My body is the frame wherein 'tis held,*
> *And perspective it is best Painter's art.*

It intrigues me that Shakespeare's direct references to plays and acting appear so sparingly in the sonnet sequence; this is the second appearance out of seven of the word "play", "stage" appears twice, and the word "actor" only once, that being in the previous sonnet. So sonnet 24 begins as a continuation of sonnet 23's acting metaphor with "mine eye hath play'd", and after the previous sonnet introduced the idea of hearing with eyes we now have a sonnet in which the eye is playing the role of a painter, suggesting that the eye is sonnet 23's "unperfect actor" and that the image it captures must be translated into words in order to be expressed well.

"Painter", in Middle English, meant both an "artist who paints pictures" and a "rope or chain that holds an anchor to a ship's side". The verb "steeld" originated in the 1580s and meant "make hard or strong like steel". Aside from the relatively straightforward reading of this line, we can also see it tie in to the established sailing theme.

"Table" was a loaded term meaning "piece of furniture with a flat top and legs", "board", "slab", "plate", "writing tablet", "gaming table" and, most interestingly, "arrangement of numbers or other figures on a tabular surface for convenience".

The word table appears only three times in the sequence, and whereas here the table is "of my heart", in sonnet 122 the tables are "within my brain".

In Old English "body" meant "trunk of a man or beast", "physical structure of a human or animal", "material frame", "material existence of a human", or "main or principal part of anything", and it maintained most of its meaning through to Shakespeare's day by which it had picked up an additional "any number of individuals spoken of collectively". As the 154 sonnets are spoken of (and for) collectively, it seems that this last meaning is quite apt.

"Frame", meaning "border or case for a picture or pane of glass", only originated half a century after Shakespeare's death, but in his day it included "a structure composed according to a plan", "enclosing border" and "profit", "benefit" or "advancement", all of which can refer to the sonnet sequence following the established themes.

"Perspective" meant the "science of optics", and the "art of drawing objects so as to give appearance of distance or depth".

In the Arden Sonnets, Katherine Duncan-Jones suggests that this might be a reference to "perspective glass", "an optical instrument for seeing things not accessible to normal view", but I've had a hard time corroborating that as the only mentions of "perspective glass" I've found are from after the year that the sonnets were first published.

There are a number of ways of reading the word "best" in "it is best Painter's art", but I believe that the key to reading it correctly is in the capitalisation of the word "Painter", which is not capitalised in the first line. This suggests that Shakespeare's eye, the sonnet, is playing the role of a painter and when in that role is referred to by the proper noun "Painter", although of course "Painter" could also refer to Shakespeare himself; with this is mind, "best Painter's art" has the word "best" describing "Painter", and so "perspective", the art of creating the illusion of the depth of Shakespeare's spirit, is the art of "best Painter".

In the first quatrain, then, the sonnet sequence appears to be speaking to Shakespeare, saying "this sonnet has taken on the role of painter and has reinforced the memory of Shakespeare's form in the arrangement of its pages; the majority of the sonnet text is the frame in which Shakespeare's memory is held, and creating the illusion of the depth of Shakespeare's spirit is its art".

> *For through the Painter must you see his skill,*
> *To find where your true Image pictured lies,*
> *Which in my bosom's shop is hanging still,*
> *That hath his windows glazed with thine eyes:*

In addition to "ability" and "cleverness", "skill" also meant "power of discernment".

As noted in the Arden Sonnets: "through the painter" means "both by means of the painter and, more literally, through the painter-poet, whose eye is transparent". In this case, the skill of Shakespeare was in painting words, and only through them can we see what he was truly made of.

Image is the second word to be capitalised in sonnet 24, just as it was in sonnet 3, and meant "artificial representation that looks like a person or thing" and "reflection in a mirror". As these reflections of Shakespeare are imbued with their own perspectives and personalities, it makes sense that they would be identified by proper nouns. The "true Image", of course, is Shakespeare, but it is also possible to read lines 5 and 6 as saying "if you want to find the image of yourself, the reader that Shakespeare imagined, you must see it through his art". Considering the distinction between the "you" and "your" of these two lines and the "thee" and "thou" of the rest of the sonnet, this appears to be a viable reading.

As today, "lie" meant both "rest" and "speak falsely", so "To finde where your true Image pictur'd lies" reads "find where the real image of Shakespeare rests" as well as "find where the true image that's portrayed is untruthful", which takes us back to sonnet 17 which discusses manipulating the truth in order to seem truthful and reminding us that sonnets 23 and 24 are about acting, or pretending to be something one is not.

"Bosom" meant "breast", "womb", "surface", or "ship's hold", and "shop" meant "workshop". Since the first sonnets I have suggested that the pages of the sonnets are wombs in which Shakespeare plants the seeds of his imagination: Shakespeare's "bosom's shop" would be the place where he manufactures his emotions and imagination, each sonnet's text is a shop that produces images for the reader.

"A ship's hold" would be the second sailing reference of this sonnet, and it would be the right place for Shakespeare to store his treasure.

"Hanging still" is interesting because aside from the image evoked of a picture hanging in a workshop, it also evokes an image of a man hanging from the gallows. Either way, the image will last forever as it has been captured in the text of the sonnet and stored on the eternal page, which is Shakespeare's workshop.

I don't know what drove me to look up the word "window", but I was surprised to discover that it originated from the Old Norse "wind eye" and replaced the Old English "eye-hole" and "eye-door". Originally, it meant "an unglazed hole in a roof", so being able to read this line as "that has his unglazed holes, glazed with your eyes" would make it very interesting indeed, even more so when considering that "wind" and "breath" are mentioned frequently throughout the sequence as the reader is supposed to be lending their breath to the sonnets as they read out loud; this is further confirmation that a window, or wind eye, would refer to a sonnet.

As "glaze" meant "to fit with glass" and "glass" is used in the sequence to refer to the sonnet mirror that reflects Shakespeare's image (as well as the glassy spring in which Narcissus sees himself) we can now read this last line as "my breast, which has windows made up of my eyes".

> *Now see what good-turns eyes for eyes have done,*
> *Mine eyes have drawn thy shape, and thine for me*
> *Are windows to my breast, where-through the Sun*
> *Delights to peep, to gaze therein on thee*

The third quatrain brings all the conceits of the first two quatrains together.

"Good-turns" might refer to page turns, and it's important to note that the spelling of the two "eyes" in the original quarto text are different: as I've mentioned before, "eyes" appears to refer to Shakespeare's and the reader's eyes whereas "eies" would refer to the sonnets.

I've scanned through the original quarto text of the sonnet sequence, and out of the 14 times the word "sun" appears it is capitalised 10 times, whereas of the 3 times "son" appears it is only capitalised once. I'm confident that this is for emphasis, though precisely the intention behind the emphasis is difficult to ascertain; I strongly suspect it's to differentiate between the regular use of those words from when they refer to Hamnet and the sonnets. "The sun" could also refer to Shakespeare's creative strength and power, or the light that pours onto the page whenever the reader opens the book of sonnets.

"Peep" meant a glance through a small opening.

With Shakespeare speaking to the sonnets, he is saying that his eyes have done the sonnets favours, drawing their shape, and for Shakespeare, the sonnets are windows to Shakespeare's breast, through which the sun (his son) looks back out.

If he is speaking to the reader, then he is saying that his eyes have drawn the reader's shape, and the reader's eyes are windows to his soul, windows through which Hamnet - or the sonnets - delight to look back out.

> *Yet eyes this cunning want to grace their art*
> *They draw but what they see, know not the heart.*

The Arden Sonnets introduces sonnet 24 by saying: "By looking closely into the speaker's eye, the young man can see a perfect image of himself, his own eyes being like a glass window; but he cannot see how much the poet loves him".

For lines 11 and 12 it says: "The sun, in love with the young man, enjoys gazing out of his eyes and into those of the poet, in order to see the youth's reflected image. Behind the conceit lies the notion that the speaker loves the young man so much that 'the sun shines out of his eyes'; there may also be a side glance at the youth's role as son, not father, as in sonnets 1-17".

These comments amaze me, and the reason for my amazement is that, like in so many other instances, they touch so remarkably close to home but somehow still fail to come together and actually make it there.

In sonnet 24, what we have is the sonnet, which is Shakespeare's eye, capturing Shakespeare's beautiful form and framing its essence; through the words of the sonnet you can see Shakespeare's artistic ability, which more than any picture is where his true representation lies.

These words remain on display on this page in the bosom of the sonnet sequence, and these pages are like windows glazed with the reader's eyes. Now see how the sonnet's and the reader's eyes compensate one another: Shakespeare has drawn the sonnet's shape, the sonnets serve as the windows to his soul through which the reader's eyes delight to look in and through which the memory of Hamnet looks out. For all this, though, the reader's eyes take in only what they see, and the image they paint in their hearts could never be quite the same as the inner-workings of the bard's mind.

SONNET 25

1609 QUARTO VERSION

LEt thoſe who are in fauor with their ſtars,
Of publike honour and proud titles boſt,
Whilſt I whome fortune of ſuch tryumph bars
Vnlookt for ioy in that I honour moſt;
Great Princes fauorites their fair leaues ſpread,
But as the Marygold at the ſuns eye,
And in them-ſelues their pride lies buried,
For at a frowne they in their glory die.
The painefull warrier famoſed for worth,
After a thouſand victories once foild,
Is from the booke of honour raſed quite,
And all the reſt forgot for which he toild:
Then happy I that loue and am beloued
Where I may not remoue, nor be remoued.

ANALYSIS

Before we begin to discuss the sonnet itself, I feel obligated to draw attention to the number 24, which I feel certain should be important considering that there are 24 hours in a day.

> *Let those who are in favour with their stars,*
> *Of public honour and proud titles boast,*
> *Whilst I whom fortune of such triumph bars*
> *Unlook'd for joy in that I honour most;*

"To be in favour with one's stars" means to enjoy success and good fortune. Additionally, throughout the sonnet sequence "stars" refers to the eyes of Shakespeare's reflection, just as they refer to the eyes of Narcissus' reflection in Ovid's Metamorphoses.

"Honour" meant "glory", "renown", "fame earned", "dignity", "distinction", "position", "victory", "triumph", "splendor", "beauty" and "excellence".

"Titles" meant "name showing a person's rank", but that was a relatively new definition in Shakespeare's day and originally meant "inscription", "heading" and "name of a book or play".

"Tryumph" bears the military connotation of "success in battle" or "conquest", but also "spiritual victory", both of which are appropriate as the sequence is Shakespeare's attempt to fill the "trenches" of the sonnet pages with his spirit which will from there infiltrate the reader's mind.

"Bars" is understood to mean "prevents", but could also have been understood to mean "imprisons". This ties into the theme of sonnet 5's "liquid prisoner" in which Shakespeare's spirit is imprisoned in the text of the page.

"Joy" meant "pleasure", "delight", "erotic pleasure", "bliss" or "joyfulness", but from the 1580s was also a term of endearment, so we can read this as either a verb or a noun.

The first quatrain of sonnet 25 is intriguing because it can be read in two startlingly contradictory ways. The well-understood interpretation is that Shakespeare is barred from enjoying the triumph of public honour and titles, unlike those who are born under the right stars; at the same time, the sonnets will always be in favour with their stars, Shakespeare's eyes, and this presents us with two alternative readings: the first in which "joy" is "unlooked for", and the second wherein "unlooked for" qualifies the "I" of "whilst I, unlooked for, whom fortune of such triumph bars".

If it is "joy" that is unlooked for, then Shakespeare is triumphing in what he honours most, the sonnets, which takes precedence over joy: this reading is borne out by the later sonnets who complain of the unfairness of their entire existence being directed towards mourning their lost love.

If "I" is the subject of "unlooked for", then Shakespeare himself would be the "unlooked for joy" and his triumph would be in capturing himself in his sonnets, which he honours most. If this is the case, then it predicts the centuries in which we've been hunting exclusively for Shakespeare's supposed lover rather than for the Bard himself.

> *Great Princes' favourites their fair leaves spread,*
> *But as the Marigold at the Sun's eye,*
> *And in them-selves their pride lies buried,*
> *For at a frown they in their glory die.*

The capitalised "Princes" recalls the princes of sonnet 14. According to the Arden Sonnets, "princes" in Elizabethan usage could be female or male, which takes us back to the "master mistress" of sonnet 20.

"Favourite" meant "person or thing regarded with especial liking", but in Shakespeare's day also meant "a person who gains dominant influence over a superior".

Considering the connections between Hamnet and Hamlet, and

Hamnet and the sonnets, I suspect that Shakespeare or Hamnet may be considered "great princes" and the favourites would have been the sonnets.

As I've discussed before, "fair" was likely intended to carry the additional meaning of "artificial" from the Old French "faire".

"Marigold at the Sun's eye" may be a reference to the Narcissus flower, which has a golden corona in the centre.

"Marygold" is capitalised, and the only related story I could find in Ovid's Metamorphoses was that of King Midas.

After Bacchus granted King Midas his wish to turn everything he touched into gold, the king is described as "Rejoycing in his harme away full merye", and later Phoebus punishes him with asses ears for having poor taste in music, which is clearly the inspiration for Bottom's transformation in "A Midsummer Night's Dream".

I've read elsewhere the story that Midas' daughter was named Zoe, or Marygold, and was accidentally turned into gold by her father, but that version is not from Ovid and so I cannot be sure of Shakespeare's familiarity with it, just as I've found a story about "Caltha" staring at Phoebus and melting into a marigold, but I've no idea where these stories come from or how far back they originated. The marigold also happens to be the flower of Dia de Meurtos, or Dia de los Meurtos, which I'm fairly confident Shakespeare would not have been familiar with.

The symbolism of flowers also poses difficulties when it comes to discovering their origins, and although I've read online that marigold symbolises cruelty, grief, jealousy, and passion, which suit the sonnets well, I'm unable to verify that any of them would have been familiar to the English in the 16th and 17th centuries.

The Arden Sonnets states that "The acknowledged characteristic of the Elizabethan marigold ... was that it opened and closed in response to the sun". As discussed in the previous episode, "The sun" could refer to the light that pours onto the page whenever the reader opens the book of sonnets. Here, this happens when the leaves (pages) are spread open, and just like the marigold flower they are buried amongst themselves whenever the sun ceases to shine (the reader closes the book).

The only other plausible meaning I can take from "Marygold" was that early Christians originally put flowers on Mary's alter in place of coins, hence its name. Apparently in Victorian times the flower represented a desire for riches due to its association with coins, so perhaps there's some relevance here with the already established themes of status, of graves and of alchemical gold.

In the Arden Sonnets, Katherine Duncan-Jones connects this quatrain with sonnet 1's "within thine own bud buriest thy content", which seems apt.

What all that background tells us about the second quatrain is that in addition to a straightforward reading of "those lucky few have only a short time to enjoy their good fortune", we can also read "Shakespeare's favourites, the sonnets, spread their pages but only live gloriously as long as they entertain the reader".

> *The painful warrior famoused for worth,*
> *After a thousand victories once foiled,*
> *Is from the book of honour razed quite,*
> *And all the rest forgot for which he toiled:*

"Painful warrior" is an important term, as painful meant full of "difficulty", "woe", "suffering" or "punishment" from the Old French, and "warrior" is a continuation of the established military theme.

"Famoused" appears to have meant "made famous", and "worth" meant "value", "price", "price paid", "worthiness" or "merit".

It astounds me that many critics and publishers have replaced one or other of the words "worth" and "quite" simply because they don't rhyme, as if with all the care he took in the production of the sonnets the Bard wouldn't have noticed. I cannot help but wonder if the "thousand victories" might be the successful rhymes that precede this quatrain and this one "mistake" illustrated here erases this history of success; this theory is validated by the comment in the Arden Sonnets: "It is possible that Shakespeare, never a brilliant rhymester, left these lines imperfect". I can't tell whether or not Katherine Duncan-Jones intended this statement to be ironic considering just how cleverly and consistently he rhymes throughout all his works.

"Foiled" is interesting because we automatically read it as "to be defeated", but it also meant "leaf", "foliage", "sheet of paper", or "sheet of metal" from the Old French and from the 1580's carried the sense of "one who enhances another by contrast". Combined with the use of the word "rased" which can be read as either "erased" or "to be raised up", this provides another contrasting reading for the third quatrain.

On the surface, the third quatrain appears to be a reference to some known tale or an amalgamation of known tales, and tells the story of how a single mistake can destroy one's reputation and legacy. Bearing in mind that Shakespeare never published any of his plays, we can also read it as follows: "once Shakespeare - the sorrowful warrior famed for his many victories as a playwright - has been embedded in the pages of the sequence, he will be raised up from this book of honour, and those plays and everything else that he worked for would quickly be forgotten, at least for the duration of the reading".

Then happy I that love and am beloved
Where I may not remove, nor be removed.

"Remove" meant "move", "take away" or "dismiss" from the Old French "move", "stir", "leave", "depart" or "take away".

In the traditional reading, Shakespeare is not like those lucky high-borns, and must seek his fortune elsewhere; those princes and favourites are doomed to lose everything at their first signs of being unworthy. Still, Shakespeare is happy to love and be loved by his sonnets, where, once published, his existence, his reputation, and his love will be fixed for all eternity.

In the alternative reading that I'm proposing here, Shakespeare enjoys his own triumphs, the sonnets, but they, like great prince's favourites, only get to enjoy the sun as long as they're enjoyed by their readers. Once Shakespeare wraps his spirit with the pages and words of the sonnets, his buried pride will be raised from this honoured book and the reader will forget everything but the world that the sonnet describes: the sonnets will be happy that they both love and are loved from a place in which they are fixed and motionless and cannot be removed.

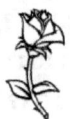

THANKS

I have many teachers, authors and people to be grateful for in the production of this material.

First and foremost, my lecturer and advisor Dr Noam Reisner of Tel Aviv University, whose love for the Bard is infectious and whose knowledge, wisdom and manner are thoroughly inspiring.

I am grateful for and owe an honourable mention to certain other members of the English Department as well, for their lessons and their support in my studies, in particular Prof. Shirley Sharon-Zisser, Prof. Elana Gomel, and Prof. Karen Alkalay-Gut.

To all of those who've come before me. I've read a lot of amazing material over the years and while the premise of my thesis may be mine, so much of what I'm saying is informed by their incredible insights and observations that I would be remiss if I didn't mention here that a lot of what I'm saying is either derivative or entirely borrowed: in particular, much thanks to Stephen Booth, Katherine Duncan-Jones, and Helen Vendler.

To the operators of **shakespeares-sonnets.com**, **openlibrary.org** and **archive.org**: you make the world a better place.

Finally, and enormously importantly: to my wife Ariane for her constant and whole-hearted support in this project, and to my son, my Phoenix, with whom I am privileged to share the love that Shakespeare's Sonnets teaches.

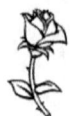

APPENDIX

The story of Narcissus and Echo as translated by Arthur Golding with side by side modern English translation

"Shakespeare's Ovid: being Arthur Golding's translation of the Metamorphoses" can be found at **http://archive.org/details/shakespearesovid00oviduoft** and **openlibrary.org**. As noted in the introduction, it's the canonical edition for any Shakespeare enthusiast.

Page 71

Original	Modernised	
The first that of his soothfast wordes had proufe in all the Realme,	The first in all the realm to receive proof of the truth of his words	
Was freckled Lyriop, whom sometime surprised in his streame,	Was freckled Lyriop, who was once taken by surprise in Cephisus' waters	
The floud Cephisus did enforce. This Lady bare a sonne	The flood god took her by force, and the lady bore him a son	
Whose beautie at his	whose beauty from birth	430

verie birth might justly love have wonne.	justly deserved all love.
Narcissus did she call his name. Of whom the Prophet sage	She called him Narcissus, and asked the wise Prophet
Demaunded if the childe should live to many yeares of age,	if the child would live many years,
Made aunswere, yea full long, so that him selfe he doe not know.	And he answered, Yes, a long life, as long as he does not know himself.
The Soothsayers wordes seemde long but vaine, untill the end did show	The Soothsayer's words seemed profound but empty, until the end of the story showed
His saying to be true in deede by straungenesse of the rage,	His prediction to be true indeed by the strangeness of Narcissus' madness,
And straungenesse of the kinde of death that did abridge his age	And the strangeness of the kind of death that cut his life short
For when yeares three times five and one he fully lyved had,	For when he had lived sixteen years,
So that he seemde to stande beetwene the	So that he appeared to be between the stages of

state of man and Lad,	man and boy,	
The hearts of divers trim yong men his beautie gan to move,	His beauty began to move the hearts of many young men,	
And many a Ladie fresh and faire was taken in his love.	And many fresh and fair ladies fell in love with him.	440
But in that grace of Natures gift such passing pride did raigne,	But in light of Nature's gift to him such pride did reign,	
That to be toucht of man or Mayde he wholy did disdaine.	That he wholly disdained the touch of any man or maiden.	
A babling Nymph that Echo hight : who hearing others talke,	A babbling Nymph named Echo : who hearing others talk,	
By no meanes can restraine hir tongue but that it needes must walke,	Could by no means restrain her tongue,	
Nor of hir selfe hath powre to ginne to speake to any wight,	nor had the power to begin speaking to anyone,	
Espyde him dryving into toyles the fearefull stagges of flight.	Spied him driving fearful stags into snares.	
This Echo was a body	This Echo had a body	

Original	Modernised	
then and not an onely voyce,	then and was not only a voice,	
Yet of hir speach she had that time no more than now the choyce,	Yet of her speech she had at that time no more choice than now,	
That is to say of many wordes the latter to repeate.	That is to say of how many words to repeat.	
The cause thereof was Junos wrath. For when that with the feate	The cause thereof was Juno's wrath. For whenever with action	450
She might have often taken Jove in daliance with his Dames,	She might have caught Jove dallying with his Dames,	
And that by stealth and unbewares in middes of all his games:	his victims usually taken by stealth and unaware in the midst of all his games:	

Page 72

Original	Modernised	
This elfe would with hir tatling talke deteine hir by the way,	This elf with her prattling talk would detain her,	
Untill that Jove had wrought his will and they were fled away.	Until Jove had had his way and they had fled.	

The which when Juno did perceyve, she said with wrathfull mood,	When Juno perceived this, she angrily said,	
This tongue that hath deluded me shall doe thee little good:	This tongue that has deceived me shall do you little good:	
For of thy speach but simple use hereafter shalt thou have.	For you will only have simple use of your speech from now on.	
The deede it selfe did straight confirme the threatnings that she gave.	Her punishment was immediately confirmed.	
Yet Echo of the former talke doth double oft the ende	So Echo often repeats the end of the previous speech	
And backe againe with just report the wordes earst spoken sende.	And returns precisely the words first spoken.	460
Now when she sawe Narcissus stray about the Forrest wyde,	Now when she saw Narcissus moving about the wide Forest,	
She waxed warme and step for step fast after him she hyde.	She blushed warmly and hurriedly followed in his footsteps.	
The more she followed after him and neerer that she came,	The more she followed him the nearer she came,	

The whoter ever did she waxe as neerer to hir flame.	The hotter she became as if from being nearer to her flame.	
Lyke as the lively Brimstone doth which dipt about a match,	Just like lively Brimstone does when a match is dipped in it,	
And put but softly to the fire, the flame doth lightly catch.	And is gently put into the fire, the flame lightly catches.	
O Lord how often would she faine (if nature would have let)	O Lord how often would she have (if nature would have let her)	
Entreated him with gentle wordes some favour for to get?	Entreated him with gentle words for some of his favour?	
But nature would not suffer hir nor give hir leave to ginne.	But nature would not go easy on her nor let her begin.	
Yet (so farre forth as she by graunt at natures hande could winne)	So (as far as she could get nature to grant her)	470
Ay readie with attentive eare she harkens for some sounde,	She readied herself with attentive ears to listen for some sound,	
Whereto she might replie hir wordes, from which she is not	Whereby she might reply with his words, from which she was not	

bounde.	prevented.	
By chaunce the stripling being strayde from all his companie,	By chance the young man was separated from all his friends,	
Sayde : is there any bodie nie? straight Echo answerde : I.	And said : is there anybody near me? straight away Echo answered : Me.	
Amazde he castes his eye aside, and looketh round about,	Amazed he cast his eyes about, and looked around,	
And come (that all the Forrest roong) aloud he calleth out.	Then come! (so that all the forest rung) aloud he called out.	
And come (sayth she :) he looketh backe, and seeing no man followe,	Then come (said she :) he looked back, and seeing no man following,	
Why fliste, he cryeth once againe : and she the same doth hallowe.	Why do you avoid me, he cried once again : and she the same did repeat.	
He still persistes, and wondring much what kinde of thing it was	He still persists, and wondering what kind of thing it was	
From which that answering voyce by turne so duely seemde to passe,	That produced that answering voice each time,	480
Sayd : let us joyne. She	Said : let us join. She (by	

(by hir will desirous to have said,	her will desirous to say,	
In fayth with none more willingly at any time or stead)	In faith with none more willingly at any time or place)	
Sayd: let us joyne. And standing somewhat in hir owne conceit,	Said: let us join. And somewhat falling under the spell of her own trick,	
Upon these wordes she left the Wood, and forth she yeedeth streit,	Upon these words she left the Wood, and went straight,	
To coll the lovely necke for which she longed had so much.	To throw her arms upon the lovely neck for which she had longed so much.	
He runnes his way, and will not be imbraced of no such.	He runs away, and will not be embraced by any such as she.	
And sayth: I first will die ere thou shalt take of me thy pleasure.	And says: I would rather die before you take pleasure from me.	
She answerde nothing else thereto, but take of me thy pleasure.	She answered nothing but, take pleasure from me.	
Now when she saw hir selfe thus mockt, she gate hir to the Woods,	Now when she saw herself mocked thus, she returned to the Woods,	
And hid hir head for	And hid her head for very	490

verie shame among the leaves and buddes.	shame among the leaves and buds.	
And ever sence she lyves alone in dennes and hollow Caves.	And ever since she lives alone in dens and hollow Caves.	
Yet stacke hir love still to hir heart, through which she dayly raves	Yet love still sticks to her heart, through which she daily raves	
The more for sorrowe of repulse. Through restlesse carke and care	The more for the sorrow of being repulsed. Through restless strain and worry	
Hir bodie pynes to skinne and bone, and waxeth wonderous bare.	Her body wastes away to skin and bone, and becomes wondrously bare.	
The bloud doth vanish into ayre from out of all hir veynes,	The blood vanishes into the air from out of her veins,	
And nought is left but voyce and bones: the voyce yet still remaynes:	And nothing is left but voice and bones: the voice yet still remains:	
Hir bones they say were turnde to stones. From thence she lurking still	Her bones they say were turned to stones. From that time onwards she still lurks	
In Woods, will never	In Woods, and never shows	

Original	Modernised	
shewe hir head in field nor yet on hill.	her head in fields or on hills.	
Yet is she heard of every man: it is hir onely sound,	Yet she is heard by every man: it is her only sound,	
And nothing else that doth remayne alive above the ground.	And nothing else remains alive above the ground.	500
Thus had he mockt this wretched Nymph and many mo beside,	So had he mocked this wretched Nymph and many more besides,	
That in the waters, Woods, and groves, or Mountaynes did abide.	That lived in the waters, Woods, and groves, or Mountains.	
Thus had he mocked many men. Of which one, miscontent	So had he mocked many men. Of which one, unhappy	

Page 73

Original	Modernised	
To see himselfe deluded so, his handes to Heaven up bent,	To find himself thwarted so, raised his hands to Heaven,	
And sayd: I pray to God he may once feele fierce Cupids fire	And said: I pray to God that he may feel fierce Cupid's fire	
As I doe now, and yet not	As I do now, but not the	

joy the things he doth desire.	joy of what he desires.	
The Goddesse Ramnuse (who doth wrealce on wicked people take)	The Goddesse Ramnuse (who takes vengeance on wicked people)	
Assented to his just request for ruth and pities sake.	Agreed to his fair request out of pity.	
There was a Spring withouten mudde as silver cleare and still,	There was a Spring without mud as clear and still as silver,	
Which neyther sheepeheirds, nor the Goates that fed upon the hill,	Which neither shepherds, nor the Goats that fed on the hill,	510
Nor other cattell troubled had, nor savage beast had styrd,	Nor any other cattle had troubled, nor any savage beast had stirred,	
Nor braunch, nor sticke, nor leafe of tree, nor any foule nor byrd.	Nor branch, nor stick, nor leaf of any tree, nor any birds.	
The moysture fed and kept aye fresh the grasse that grew about,	The moisture fed and kept the grass that grew around it fresh,	
And with their leaves the trees did keepe the heate of Phoebus out.	And with their leaves the trees kept the heat of Phoebus out.	
The stripling wearie with	The young man weary	

the heate and hunting in the chace,	from the heat and from giving chase while hunting,	
And much delighted with the spring and coolenesse of the place,	And much delighted with the spring and the coolness of the place,	
Did lay him downe upon the brimme : and as he stooped lowe	Did lie down upon the edge of the water : and as he stooped low	
To staunche his thurst, another thurst of worse effect did growe.	To staunch his thirst, another far worse thirst grew.	
For as he dranke, he chaunst to spie the Image of his face,	For as he drank, he happened to see the Image of his face,	
The which he did immediately with fervent love embrace.	Which he immediately embraced with fervent love.	520
He feedes a hope without cause why. For like a foolishe noddie	He fuels a hope without a cause. For like a foolish child	
He thinkes the shadow that he sees, to be a lively boddie.	He believes the shadow that he sees, to be a live body.	
Astraughted like an ymage made of Marble stone he lyes,	Frozen like an image made of Marble stone he lies,	

There gazing on his shadow still with fixed staring eyes.	There gazing on his still shadow with transfixed staring eyes.	
Stretcht all along upon the ground, it doth him good to see	Stretched along the ground, it does him good to see	
His ardent eyes which like two starres full bright and shyning bee,	His ardent eyes which are bright and shining like two stars,	
And eke his fingars, fingars such as Bacchus might beseeme,	And also his fingers, fingers such as might suit Bacchus,	
And haire that one might worthely Apollos haire it deeme.	And hair that one might worthily deem Apollo's.	
His beardlesse chinne and yvorie necke, and eke the perfect grace	His beardless chin and ivory neck, and also the perfect grace	
Of white and red indifFerently bepainted in his face.	Of white and red indifFerently painted on his face.	530
All these he woondreth to beholde, for which (as I doe gather)	All these he wondered to behold, for which (as I gather)	
Himselfe was to be wondred at, or to be pitied rather.	He himself was to be wondered at, or rather to be pitied.	

He is enamored of himselfe for want of taking heede.	He is enamoured of himself for lack of taking heed.	
And where he lykes another thing, he lykes himselfe in deede.	And where he likes another thing, he likes himself indeed.	
He is the partie whome he wooes, and suter that doth wooe,	He is the party whom he woo's, and the suiter that woo's,	
He is the flame that settes on fire, and thing that burneth tooe.	He is the flame that sets on fire, and the thing that burns too.	
O Lord how often did he kisse that false deceitfull thing?	O Lord how often did he kiss that false deceitful thing?	
How often did he thrust his armes midway into the spring,	How often did he thrust his arms halfway into the spring,	
To have embraste the necke he saw and could not catch himselfe?	To have embraced the neck that he saw but could not catch himself?	
He knowes not what it was he sawe. And yet the foolishe elfe	He does not know what it was he saw. And yet the foolish elf	540
Doth burne in ardent love thereof. The verie selfe same thing	Burns in ardent love thereof. The very self-same thing	

That doth bewitch and blinde his eyes, encreaseth all his sting,	That bewitches and blinds his eyes, increases the pain of its sting,	
Thou fondling thou, why doest thou raught the fickle image so?	You fond thing, why do you strike the fickle image so?	
The thing thou seekest is not there. And if a side thou go,	The thing you seek is not there. And if you move away,	
The thing thou lovest straight is gone. It is none other matter	The thing you love will disappear. It is nothing other	
That thou dost see, than of thy selfe the shadow in the water.	That you see, than the shadow of yourself in the water.	
The thing is nothing of it selfe: with thee it doth abide,	The thing is nothing in and of itself: with you it abides,	
With thee it would departe if thou withdrew thy selfe aside.	With you it would depart if you withdrew yourself.	
No care of meate could draw him thence, nor yet desire of rest.	No taste for meat could draw him from there, nor desire to rest.	
But lying flat against the ground, and leaning on his brest,	But lying flat on the ground, and leaning on his breast,	550

Original	Modernised	
With greedie eyes he gazeth still uppon the falced face,	With greedy eyes he gazes still upon the false face,	
And through his sight is wrought his bane. Yet for a little space	And through his sight is his doom wrought. Yet for a short time	
He turnes and settes him-selfe upright, and holding up his hands	He turns and sets himself upright, and holding up his hands	
With piteous voyce unto the wood that round about him stands,	With piteous voice to the wood that round about him stands,	

Page 74

Original	Modernised	
Cryes out and ses: alas ye Woods, and was there ever any,	Cries out and says: alas you Woods, was there ever any,	
That loovde so cruelly as I? you know: for unto many	That loved so cruelly as I? you know: for unto many	
A place of harbrough have you beene, and fort of refuge strong.	A place of harbour have you been, and strong forts of refuge.	
Can you remember any one in all your tyme so long,	Can you remember anyone in all your time so long,	

That hath so pinde away as I? I see and am full faine,	That has so pined away as I? I see and am fully joyful,	
Howbeit that I like and see I cannot yet attaine:	How is it that I like and see and yet cannot attain:	560
So great a blindnesse in my heart through doting love doth raigne.	So great a blindness reigns in my heart through doting love.	
And for to spight me more withall, it is no journey farre,	And to spite me more withal, it is no far journey,	
No drenching Sea, no Mountaine hie, no wall, no locke, no barre,	No drenching Sea, no Mountain high, no wall, no lock, no bar,	
It is but even a little droppe that keepes us two asunder.	It is but a little drop that keeps us two apart.	
He would be had. For looke how oft I kisse the water under,	He would be had. For look how often I kiss the water,	
So oft againe with upwarde mouth he ryseth towarde mee,	So often again with upturned mouth he rises towards me,	
A man would thinke to touch at least I should yet able bee.	A man would think I should at least be able to touch.	
It is a trifle in respect	It seems just a trifle that	

that lettes us of our love.	keeps us from our love.	
What wight soever that thou art come hither up above.	Whatever man you are come here up above.	
O pierlesse piece, why dost thou mee thy lover thus delude?	O peerless piece, why do you evade me your lover?	570
Or whither fliste thou of thy friende thus earnestly pursude?	Or why do you avoid your friend when so earnestly pursued?	
Iwis I neyther am so fowle nor yet so growne in yeares,	Certainly I am neither so foul nor so old,	
That in this wise thou shouldst me shoon. To have me to their Feeres,	That in this way you should shun me. To be my consorts,	
The Nymphes themselves have sude ere this. And yet (as should appeere)	The Nymphs themselves have sued before this. And yet (as it appears)	
Thou dost pretende some kinde of hope of friendship by the cheere.	You pretend some kind of hope of friendship by your face.	
For when I stretch mine armes to thee, thou stretchest thine likewise,	For when I stretch my arms to you, you stretch yours likewise,	

And if I smile thou smilest too: And when that from mine eyes	And if I smile you smile too: And when from my eyes	
The teares doe drop, I well perceyve the water stands in thine.	The tears drop, I see well that the water stands in yours.	
Like gesture also dost thou make to everie becke of mine.	You make similar gestures to every beckoning of mine.	
And as by moving of thy sweete and lovely lippes I weene,	And by the moving of your sweet and lovely lips I see,	580
Thou speakest words although mine eares conceive not what they beene.	You speak words although my ears cannot hear what you say.	
It is my selfe I well perceyve, it is mine Image sure,	It is myself I see well, it is my own Image surely,	
That in this sort deluding me, this furie doth procure.	That in this manner evades me, generates this fury.	
I am inamored of my selfe, I doe both set on fire,	I am enamoured of myself, I both set on fire,	
And am the same that swelteth too, through impotent desire.	And am the same that is burned too, through impotent desire.	

What shall I doe ? be woode or wo ? whome shall I wo therefore ?	What shall I do ? be woo'ed or woo ? whom shall I woo therefore ?	
The thing I seeke is in my selfe, my plentie makes me poore.	The thing I seek is in myself, my plenty makes me poor.	
O would to God I for a while might from my bodie part.	O I would to God that for a while I might from my body be apart.	
This wish is straunge to heare a Lover wrapped all in smart,	This wish is strange to hear a Lover wrapped in hurt,	
To wish away the thing the which he loveth as his heart.	Wishing away the thing that he loves as his heart.	590
My sorrowe takes away my strength. I have not long to live,	My sorrow takes away my strength. I have not long to live,	
But in the floure of youth must die. To die it doth not grieve,	But in the flower of youth I must die. Dying would not be cause to grieve,	
For that by death shall come the ende of all my griefe and paine.	Because by death shall come the end of all my grief and pain.	
I woulde this yongling whome I love might lenger life obtaine:	I wish that this young man whom I love might a longer life obtain:	

For in one soule shall now delay we stedfast Lovers twaine.	For in one soul we two steadfast Lovers are now detained.	
This saide in rage he turnes againe unto the foresaide shade,	This said in rage he turns again to the aforementioned shade,	
And rores the water with the teares and sloubring that he made,	And roughs the water with his tears and his slobbering,	
That through his troubling of the Well his ymage gan to fade.	That through his troubling of the Well his image began to fade.	
Which when he saw to vanish so, Oh whither dost thou flie?	Which when he saw it vanishing so, Oh where do you fly?	
Abide I pray thee heartely, aloud he gan to crie.	Stay I pray you heartily, aloud he began to cry.	600
Forsake me not so cruelly that loveth thee so deere,	Do not forsake so cruelly he who loves you so dearly,	
But give me leave a little while my dazled eyes to cheere	But give me leave a little while to cheer my dazzled eyes	
With sight of that which for to touch is utterly denide,	With the sight of that for which touch is utterly denied,	

Thereby to feede my wretched rage and furie for a tide.	Thereby to feed my wretched rage and fury for a time.	
As in this wise he made his mone, he stripped off his cote	And in this way he moaned, he stripped off his coat	

Page 75

Original	Modernised	
And with his fist outragiously his naked stomacke smote.	And with his fist excessively struck his naked stomach.	
A ruddie colour where he smote rose on his stomacke sheere,	Where he struck on his stomach a ruddy colour rose sheer,	
Lyke Apples which doe partly white and striped red appeere.	Like Apples which are partly white and striped red appear.	
Or as the clusters ere the grapes to ripenesse fully come:	Or as the clusters of grapes before they're fully ripened:	
An Orient purple here and there beginnes to grow on some.	An Orient purple here and there begins to grow on some.	610
Which things assoone as in the spring he did beholde againe,	Which things as soon as saw again in his reflection in the spring,	

He could no longer beare it out. But fainting straight for paine,	He could no longer bear it. But fainted immediately from the pain,	
As lith and supple waxe doth melt against the burning flame,	As lithe and supple wax melts against the burning flame,	
Or morning dewe against the Sunne that glareth on the same:	Or morning dew against the Sun that glares on the same:	
Even so by piecemale being spent and wasted through desire,	Being spent and wasted through desire, just like that piece by piece	
Did he consume and melt away with Cupids secret fire.	Was he consumed and melted away by Cupid's secret fire.	
His lively hue of white and red, his cheerefulnesse and strength	His lively hue of white and red, his cheerfulness and strength	
And all the things that lyked him did wanze away at length.	And all his good characteristics faded away at length.	
So that in fine remayned not the bodie which of late	So that finally the body no longer remained which of late	
The wretched Echo loved so. Who when she sawe his state,	The wretched Echo had loved so. Who when she saw his state,	620

Although in heart she angrie were, and mindefull of his pride,	Although in heart she was angry, and mindful of his pride,	
Yet ruing his unhappie case, as often as he cride	Yet ruing his unhappy case, as often as he cried	
Alas, she cride alas likewise with shirle redoubled sound.	Alas, she cried alas likewise with shrill redoubled sound.	
And when he beate his breast, or strake his feete agaynst the ground,	And when he beat his breast, or struck his feet against the ground,	
She made like noyse of clapping too. These are the wordes that last	She made the same noise of clapping too. These are the words that last	
Out of his lippes beholding still his woonted ymage past.	Out of his lips she still beholds his beloved image past.	
Alas sweete boy belovde in vaine, farewell. And by and by	Alas sweet boy loved in vain, farewell. And by and by	
With sighing sound the selfe same wordes the Echo did reply.	With sighing sound the self-same words the Echo did reply.	
With that he layde his wearie head against the grassie place,	With that he laid his weary head against the grassy place,	
And death did cloze his	And death closed his gaz-	630

gazing eyes that woondred at the grace	ing eyes that wondered at the grace
And beautie which did late adorne their Masters heavenly face.	And beauty which did late adorn their Master's heavenly face.
And afterward when into Hell receyved was his spright,	And afterwards when his spirit was received in Hell,
He goes me to the Well of Styx, and there both day and night	He went to the Well of Styx, and there both day and night
Standes tooting on his shadow still as fondely as before.	Stands gazing on his shadow still as fondly as before.
The water Nymphes his sisters wept and wayled for him sore,	The water Nymphs his sisters wept and wailed for him sorely,
And on his bodie strowde their haire dipt off and shorne therefore.	And on his body was strewn their hair that they had cut off for him.
The Woodnymphes also did lament. And Echo did rebound	The Wood nymphs lamented also. And Echo rebounded
To every sorrowfull noyse of theirs with like lamenting sound.	Every sorrowful noise of theirs with a likewise lamenting sound.
The fire was made to	The fire was made to burn

burne the corse, and waxen Tapers light.	the corpse, and waxed Tapers were lit.	
A Herce to lay the bodie on with solemne pompe was dight.	A Hearse to lay the body on was adorned with solemn pomp.	640
But as for bodie none remaind: In stead thereof they found	But as for the body none remained: Instead they found	
A yellow floure with milke white leaves new sprong upon the ground.	A yellow flower with milk-white leaves newly sprung from the ground.	
This matter all Achaia through did spreade the Prophets fame:	This matter spread the Prophet's fame all through Achaia:	
That every where of just desert renowmed was his name.	So that everywhere in justly deserving manner his name was renowned.	

Quotes and references from Narcissus and Echo in the Sonnets

The following list of examples where the sonnets reference the story of Narcissus and Echo was put together quickly and not rigorously, it is long but not exhaustive, and it doesn't really take into consideration the full implications of the surrounding text nor entire conceits that have been lifted directly. During the course of my analysis of sonnet 7 I realised that the sonnets contain direct references to many other stories as well, which remain to be explored.

Arthur Golding's Narcissus and Echo	Shakespeare's Sonnets
"I pray to God he may once feele fierce Cupids fire And said : I pray to God that he may feel fierce Cupid's fire As I doe now, and yet not joy the things he doth desire."	**Sonnet 153** "Cupid laid by his brand and fell asleep: A maid of Dian's this advantage found, And his love-kindling fire did quickly steep In a cold valley-fountain of that ground"
"The Goddesse Ramnuse (who doth wrealce on wicked people take) The	**Sonnet 14** "Nor can I fortune to brief minutes tell,

Goddesse Ramnuse (who takes vengeance on wicked people)
Assented to his just request for ruth and pities sake."

(it might be that the goddess is represented only by Fortune with a capital F)

Pointing to each his thunder, rain and wind,"

Sonnet 25

"Whilst I, whom fortune of such triumph bars
Unlook'd for joy in that I honour most."

Sonnet 29

"When in disgrace with fortune and men's eyes
I all alone beweep my outcast state,"

Sonnet 32

"And shalt by fortune once more re-survey
These poor rude lines of thy deceased lover,"

Sonnet 37

"So I, made lame by Fortune's dearest spite,
Take all my comfort of thy

worth and truth; "

Sonnet 90

"Join with the spite of fortune, make me bow,
And do not drop in for an after-loss:"

"But in the onset come: so shall I taste
At first the very worst of fortune's might;"

Sonnet 111

"O! for my sake do you with Fortune chide,
The guilty goddess of my harmful deeds,"

Sonnet 124

"If my dear love were but the child of state,
It might for Fortune's bastard be unfathered,"

"There was a Spring withouten mudde as silver cleare and still,"

(5 out of 6 references to spring refer to both the season and the water source that Narcissus saw his reflection in. It appears that the seasons refer to the personifications of seasons as described in Golding's translation of the story of Phaethon)

Sonnet 1

"Thy self thy foe, to thy sweet self too cruel: Thou that art now the world's fresh ornament, And only herald to the gaudy spring, Within thine own bud buriest thy content,"

Sonnet 35

"Roses have thorns, and silver fountains mud"

Sonnet 53

"Speak of the spring, and foison of the year, The one doth shadow of your beauty show"

(foison: harvest, plenty, abundance)

Sonnet 63

"Stealing away the treasure

	of his spring"
	Sonnet 98 "From you have I been absent in the spring,"
	Sonnet 102 "Our love was new, and then but in the spring, When I was wont to greet it with my lays" (lays: songs, poems)
"Which neyther sheepeheirds, nor the Goates that fed upon the hill, Which neither shepherds, nor the Goats that fed on the hill, Nor other cattell troubled had, nor savage beast had styrd, Nor any other cattle had troubled, nor any savage beast had stirred, Nor braunch, nor sticke, nor	**Sonnet 7** "And having climbed the steep-up heavenly hill"

leafe of tree, nor any foule nor byrd."	
"And much delighted with the spring and coolenesse of the place, And much delighted with the spring and the coolness of the place, Did lay him downe upon the brimme : and as he stooped lowe Did lie down upon the edge of the water : and as he stooped low To staunche his thurst, another thurst of worse effect did growe."	**Sonnet 154** "This brand she quenched in a cool well by, Which from Love's fire took heat perpetual" "Love's fire heats water, water cools not love."
"He feedes a hope without cause why. For like a foolishe noddie He thinkes the shadow that he sees, to be a lively boddie." (feeding, fool and shadow are	**Sonnet 1** "Feed'st thy light's flame with self-substantial fuel," **Sonnet 27** "Save that my soul's imaginary sight

referenced numerous times)	Presents thy shadow to my sightless view,"
	Sonnet 37 "So then I am not lame, poor, nor despised, Whilst that this shadow doth such substance give That I in thy abundance am sufficed, And by a part of all thy glory live." **Sonnet 43** "Then thou, whose shadow shadows doth make bright, How would thy shadow's form form happy show" **Sonnet 53** "What is your substance, whereof are you made, That millions of strange shadows on you tend?

Since every one hath, every one, one shade,
And you but one, can every shadow lend."

"Speak of the spring, and foison of the year,
The one doth shadow of your beauty show,
The other as your bounty doth appear;
And you in every blessed shape we know."

Sonnet 57

"So true a fool is love, that in your will,
Though you do anything, he thinks no ill"

Sonnet 61

"Dost thou desire my slumbers should be broken,
While shadows like to thee do mock my sight?"

	Sonnet 67
	"Why should poor beauty indirectly seek Roses of shadow, since his rose is true?"
	Sonnet 98
	"Yet seemed it winter still, and you away, As with your shadow I with these did play."
	Sonnet 116
	"Love's not Time's fool, though rosy lips and cheeks Within his bending sickle's compass come;"
	Sonnet 124
	"To this I witness call the fools of time, Which die for goodness, who have lived for crime."
	Sonnet 137

	"Thou blind fool, Love, what dost thou to mine eyes, That they behold, and see not what they see?"
	Sonnet 141 "But my five wits nor my five senses can Dissuade one foolish heart from serving thee, Who leaves unswayed the likeness of a man, Thy proud heart's slave and vassal wretch to be:"
"Astraughted like an ymage made of Marble stone he lyes,"	**Sonnet 55** "Not marble, nor the gilded monuments Of princes, shall outlive this powerful rhyme; But you shall shine more bright in these contents Than unswept stone, be-

	smear'd with sluttish time."
	Sonnet 97 "What freezings have I felt, what dark days seen!"
"His ardent eyes which like two starres full bright and shyning bee"	**Sonnet 14** "Not from the stars do I my judgement pluck; And yet methinks I have Astronomy," "But from thine eyes my knowledge I derive, And, constant stars, in them I read such art As truth and beauty shall together thrive," **Sonnet 15** "That this huge stage presenteth nought but shows Whereon the stars in secret influence comment;" **Sonnet 25**

"Let those who are in favour with their stars
Of public honour and proud titles boast,
Whilst I, whom fortune of such triumph bars
Unlook'd for joy in that I honour most."

Sonnet 26

"Till whatsoever star that guides my moving,
Points on me graciously with fair aspect,
And puts apparel on my tottered loving,
To show me worthy of thy sweet respect:"

Sonnet 28

"So flatter I the swart-complexion'd night,
When sparkling stars twire not thou gild'st the even."

	(swart: dark, twire: twinkle, gild'st: make gold)
	Sonnet 116 "It is the star to every wandering bark,"
	Sonnet 132 "Nor that full star that ushers in the even, Doth half that glory to the sober west, As those two mourning eyes become thy face:"
"Of white and red indifferently painted on his face."	**Sonnet 99** "The roses fearfully on thorns did stand, One blushing shame, another white despair; A third, nor red nor white, had stol'n of both, And to his robbery had annexed thy breath;"

	Sonnet 130 "I have seen roses damasked, red and white, But no such roses see I in her cheeks;"
"He himself was to be wondered at, or rather to be pitied."	**Sonnet 1** "Pity the world, or else this glutton be," **Sonnet 111** "Pity me, then, and wish I were renewed;" "Pity me then, dear friend, and I assure ye, Even that your pity is enough to cure me." **Sonnet 112** "Your love and pity doth the impression fill, Which vulgar scandal stamped upon my brow;"

	Sonnet 132 "Thine eyes I love, and they, as pitying me, Knowing thy heart torments me with disdain," "To mourn for me since mourning doth thee grace, And suit thy pity like in every part."
	Sonnet 140 "Lest sorrow lend me words, and words express The manner of my pity-wanting pain." **Sonnet 142** "Root pity in thy heart, that, when it grows, Thy pity may deserve to pitied be."
"He is the partie whome he	**Sonnet 35**

wooes, and suter that doth wooe,"

"For to thy sensual fault I bring in sense,
Thy adverse party is thy advocate,
And 'gainst myself a lawful plea commence:
Such civil war is in my love and hate,"

Sonnet 41

"And when a woman woos, what woman's son
Will sourly leave her till he have prevailed?
Ay me! but yet thou mightst my seat forbear,
And chide thy beauty and thy straying youth,"

Sonnet 54

"But, for their virtue only is their show,
They live unwoo'd, and unrespected fade;"

Sonnet 70

"Thy worth the greater, being wooed of time;
For canker vice the sweetest buds doth love,"

Sonnet 136

"And will, thy soul knows, is admitted there;
Thus far for love, my love-suit, sweet, fulfil."

Sonnet 142

"Be it lawful I love thee, as thou lov'st those
Whom thine eyes woo as mine importune thee:"

Sonnet 144

"To win me soon to hell, my female evil,
Tempteth my better angel from my side,
And would corrupt my saint

	to be a devil, Wooing his purity with her foul pride."
"He is the flame that sets on fire, and the thing that burns too."	**Sonnet 1** "Feed'st thy light's flame with self-substantial fuel" **Sonnet 45** "The other two, slight air and purging fire, Are both with thee, wherever I abide;" **Sonnet 73** "In me thou see'st the glowing of such fire, That on the ashes of his youth doth lie," **Sonnet 109** "Though absence seemed my flame to qualify," **Sonnet 115** "My most full flame should

	afterwards burn clearer."
	Sonnet 144 "Yet this shall I ne'er know, but live in doubt, Till my bad angel fire my good one out."
	(Sonnets 153 and 154 in general)
"O Lord how often did he kiss that false deceitful thing?"	**Sonnet 4** "Thou of thy self thy sweet self dost deceive:"
	Sonnet 39 "Which time and thoughts so sweetly doth deceive,"
	Sonnet 40 "But yet be blam'd, if thou thy self deceivest"
	Sonnet 93 "So shall I live, supposing thou art true,

	Like a deceived husband; so love's face May still seem love to me, though altered new;"
	Sonnet 104 "So your sweet hue, which methinks still doth stand, Hath motion, and mine eye may be deceived:"
"To have embraste the necke he saw and could not catch himselfe?"	**Sonnet 131** "A thousand groans, but thinking on thy face, One on another's neck, do witness bear"
"With thee it would departe if thou withdrew thy selfe aside."	**Sonnet 6** "Then what could death do if thou shouldst depart, Leaving thee living in posterity?" **Sonnet 11** "As fast as thou shalt wane,

	so fast thou grow'st In one of thine, from that which thou departest;"
	Sonnet 109 "As easy might I from my self depart As from my soul which in thy breast doth lie:"
"And through his sight is wrought his bane. Yet for a little space" (bane: doom)	**Sonnet 14** "Thy end is truth's and beauty's doom and date." **Sonnet 55** "Even in the eyes of all posterity That wear this world out to the ending doom. So, till the judgment that yourself arise, You live in this, and dwell in lovers' eyes." **Sonnet 107**

	"Can yet the lease of my true love control, Supposed as forfeit to a confined doom."
	Sonnet 116 "Love alters not with his brief hours and weeks, But bears it out even to the edge of doom."
	Sonnet 145 "Chiding that tongue that ever sweet Was used in giving gentle doom;"
"and was there ever any, That loovde so cruelly as I "	**Sonnet 1** "Thy self thy foe, to thy sweet self too cruel:" (the rest of the references are within the context of the dark mistress)

"It is a trifle in respect that lettes us of our love."	**Sonnet 48** "Each trifle under truest bars to thrust" "But thou, to whom my jewels trifles are" "That in this sort deluding me, this furie doth procure." **Sonnet 100** "Spend'st thou thy fury on some worthless song,"
"The thing I seeke is in my selfe, my plentie makes me poore."	**Sonnet 26** "Duty so great, which wit so poor as mine" **Sonnet 32** "These poor rude lines of thy deceased lover," **Sonnet 37** "So then I am not lame, poor, nor despised." **Sonnet 49**

"To leave poor me thou hast the strength of laws,"

Sonnet 51
"O! what excuse will my poor beast then find,"

Sonnet 53
"Describe Adonis, and the counterfeit
Is poorly imitated after you;"

Sonnet 67
"Why should poor beauty indirectly seek
Roses of shadow, since his rose is true?"

Sonnet 71
"Do not so much as my poor name rehearse;
But let your love even with my life decay;"

Sonnet 107

"My love looks fresh, and Death to me subscribes, Since, spite of him, I'll live in this poor rhyme,"

Sonnet 122

"That poor retention could not so much hold, Nor need I tallies thy dear love to score;"

Sonnet 125

"No; let me be obsequious in thy heart, And take thou my oblation, poor but free,"

Sonnet 128

"Whilst my poor lips which should that harvest reap,"

Sonnet 133

"But then my friend's heart let my poor heart bail;"

Sonnet 143

	"Not prizing her poor infant's discontent;"
	Sonnet 146 "Poor soul, the centre of my sinful earth, "
	Sonnet 151 "He is contented thy poor drudge to be,"
"For in one soule shall now delay we stedfast Lovers twaine."	**Sonnet 126** "She may detain, but not still keep, her treasure: Her audit (though delayed) answered must be,"
"Even so by piecemale being spent and wasted through desire,"	**Sonnet 129** "The expense of spirit in a waste of shame"
"Alas sweete boy belovde in vaine, farewell."	**Sonnet 108** "Nothing, sweet boy; but yet, like prayers divine,"
"And afterwards when his	**Sonnet 129**

spirit was received in Hell,"	"To shun the heaven that leads men to this hell."
"The water Nymphes his sisters wept and wayled for him sore, And on his bodie strowde their haire dipt off and shorne therefore. The Woodnymphes also did lament."	**Sonnet 154** "The little Love-god lying once asleep, Laid by his side his heart-inflaming brand, Whilst many nymphs that vowed chaste life to keep Came tripping by;"

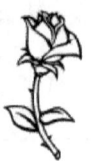

www.ingramcontent.com/pod-product-compliance
Lightning Source LLC
Chambersburg PA
CBHW071357210526
45465CB00001B/141